PRAISE FOR
VOICES OF THE 21ST CENTURY

Voices of the 21st Century contains stories of empowered women and peak experiences that enabled them to change their own lives and catalyze change in others. Key themes include: lessons learned from challenges faced, learning to listen to intuitive messages and follow your heart, and the importance of reaching out for and accepting support from others. A recommended read for women of all ages.

Pamela Thompson

What a beautiful collaboration of inspiring women from all walks of life. I found this to be truly moving, relatable, and full of applicable ways to transform my everyday life. Great read!

Tatiana Bommarito

Hearing the stories of others helps us to not feel alone with our own stories, and I am grateful to the authors for sharing theirs.

Louise Macleod

I love how relatable each of these stories is. This book is sending such a beautiful message of "If I can, you can!" No matter what your story, if you're in need of any sort of transformation, you are sure to find inspiration in this book. There's so much LOVE and LIFE in this book—highly recommend it! Just beautiful and deeply inspiring!

Marie Alessi

An excellent collection of stories and experiences.

Lee Lewis

Wow! What a celebration of extraordinary women from so many distinct and varied paths. Beautifully written, these short stories are bold yet sensitive, courageous yet vulnerable, and beautiful yet disturbing.

They ruffle feathers, and so they must, in a world that needs to change and where healing is needed. Their messages are instrumental for a new era of balance and prosperity.

Cynthia Banks

This is a powerful book that every woman should read to understand how we can achieve what we want. It is possible if we have passion. You will find amazing stories full of resilience and love for what they once dreamed of, as well as how hard they work for them. I promise you that you will fall in love with these stories of women like us with real stories that deserve to be read. I highly recommend this book.

Margarita Garcia

An inspiring collection of stories of women who endured challenges and, in turn, transformed them into empowering moments and personal growth.

Janet Corvino

This book has so many wonderful stories of empowerment. Each one has been inspiring, hopeful, and still unique to each person's story. I may not be able to fully relate to each one, but I feel they have all given me something: a smile, a feeling of empathy, a moment to remember that our stories may be different, but our struggles are human, and they are something to think about after I closed the book. I recommend this to anyone who is feeling alone, powerless, or just wants to feel a bit more connected to another woman.

Katie Slaney

This book is phenomenal! Each story presents a unique perspective and has powerful lessons between the lines. You never know how your story can touch and inspire others! I'm so happy with this purchase, and I look forward to seeing more from these courageous authors!

Jade W.

What an interesting anthology . . . the stories vary, but the voices are authentic, and all lead to a place of empowerment.

Olga Campbell

I can't recommend this book highly enough. It's full of real women telling real stories, and I'm here for that! I'll be sharing this book with others.

Tedi Dowell

This is an empowering book full of personal stories. I can't get over how brave these women are to share their stories. Each story is a quick read. In some sittings, I devoured the stories, but other times, when I sat down to read, I could only handle a couple. I needed time to process. I love a book that challenges me and inspires me to be a better person.

Jennifer Bastien

This collection of stories by women who courageously share their deeply personal and, too often, painful life experiences provides poignant examples of survival through insight, patience, and perseverance. Everyone has a story to be heard, and hopefully, these collective messages will lead all of us in the sisterhood to better listening and greater opportunity.

Karen S. Ross, PhD

I love the bits of advice throughout this book! Just one chapter a day can give you inspiration and food for thought as you navigate your world.

Kathy Dangin

These women are rock stars of so many sorts. I love the format of the book and how it flows from one impactful and hopeful story to the next. This is EXACTLY what we women need right now: guides, leaders, teachers, and sages to step forward and tell their experiences of courage and perseverance. Thank you all for bringing your story to the female transformation narrative!

D. Carter

I give this book one hundred stars! I would highly recommend this book to anyone who desires a guide on improving your mindset for a victorious life. I appreciated the advice to unlock your imagination and the emphasis on fulfilling your dreams.

Natasha Skinner

Prior to reading the excerpts within this book, I considered myself as such an overcomer of obstacles. These readings have reinvigorated the tenacity deep within me. Inspiration comes in so many forms . . . allow this to be one of yours!

Chezarae M. Slayton

Reading these inspiring stories is like talking to a close friend or family member, gaining wisdom and encouragement from each word. What an incredible way to find empowerment in this world.

Joy Villalta

To see the previous books in the ***Voices of the 21st Century*** series,

Women Who Influence, Inspire, and Make a Difference
Bold, Brave, and Brilliant Women Who Make a Difference
Powerful, Passionate Women Who Make a Difference
Resilient Women Who Rise and Make a Difference
Conscious, Caring Women Who Make a Difference
Women Transforming the World
Women Empowered through Passion and Purpose

visit
VoicesOfThe21stCenturyBook.com

VOICES OF THE 21ST CENTURY

Wise Women Bringing Light to the World

GAIL WATSON

Published by WSA Publishing
Suite 1810
1223 Wilshire Blvd.
Santa Monica. CA 90403

Copyright © 2025 by Women Speakers Association

All rights reserved. No part of this book may be reproduced or transmitted in any form or by any means, electronic or mechanical, including photocopying, recording, or by any information storage and retrieval system, without the written permission of the Publisher, except where permitted by law.

Manufactured in the United States of America, or in the United Kingdom when distributed elsewhere.

>   Watson, Gail
>   *Voices of the 21st Century: Wise Women Bringing Light to the World*
>   ISBN: 978-1-965359-00-6
>   eBook: 978-1-965359-01-3
>   LCCN: Request Pending

Copyediting: Elise Abram
Cover Design: Natasha Clawson
Interior Design: Veronika Grebennikova

Sage Awakening

Zan Johns

Our luminous light is inherent
Like the sun, we are meant to shine
Our essence is florescence
        adversity breeds wisdom
        wisdom breeds confidence
        confidence breeds adventure
        adventure breeds excellence

Bigger stories lie beneath the surface
Persistent strivers conquer each day
We routinely retreat into murky shadows
Our possibilities dawn in darkness
We faced suffering in the desert—
struggles not of our own choosing
Amid loss and despair
we dared to follow rugged paths
trekked through mud and cracks
weathered life's cyclic storms
never holding back

We gained insight from auspicious grace
Grit established tone and pace
With unyielding velocity
we cultivate our curiosity—
perceive with our hearts, ears, and eyes
Triumphant blossoms rise
We abandon turmoil and tension
Bring forth healing and inspiration

Wisdom pervades our presence—
we love boundlessly
we live authentically
we honor our roots

we fulfill our needs
we will not adhere to fear
we dream out loud
we learn from our past
we lean on faith
we lead impactfully
we care compassionately

We emerge enlightened
Reflecting every hue of the lotus—
awakened . . . pristine . . . renewed

We thank Zan Johns for capturing the essence of this book through her poetry.

Zan Johns is the world-class author of Poetic Forecast, After the Rainbow, Encore, Voices of the 21st Century *(2021–2024) and* What Matters Journal. *She's also co-editor of three poetry anthologies and an editor of* Fine Lines. *Her expressions appear in numerous publications. Zan is the poet laureate for Women Speakers Association.*

ZanExpressions.com

Contents

Foreword *by Anne-Marie Dekker* vii
Embracing Your Voice: A Journey to Belief *by Gail Watson* 1
Where Shall I Die? *by Karen Anderson* 5
Transforming Pain into Purpose—Find Your Blue Rose *by Karen Barno* 9
Conquering the Silent Saboteur of Imposter Syndrome *by Shelly L. Bell* 13
Raising Voices and Raising Capital *by Victoria Bennett* 17
More than Enough *by Dr. Renae Bjorg* 21
Caring for Kyra *by Glendoria Phillips Boyd* 25
Believing in the Transformational Power of Virtues *by Florine Clomegah-Freitas* 29
The Mephibosheth Syndrome: Restoration is Available and Comes from God *by Karen L. Collins* 33
The Power of Starting Over *by Tracy Conway* 37
Someone once Told Me that I Could Not Change The World, and for Far Too Long, I Believed Them *by TC Cooper* 41
Valentine's Day Isn't Just for Lovers: Seven Ways to Show LOVE to Your Business *by Angel Cottrell* 45
Successfully Defying Industry and Gender Stereotypes *by Karen Taylor Dade* 49
Sharing My Journey: Inspiring Others through Wellness *by Adriana D'Agostino* 53
Wisdom to Heal Emotional Pain *by Crystal Derksen* 57
It's Okay to Dream Again *by Shelly Diehm* 61
That Kid *by Jan Dunk* 65
The Wisdom to Know Yourself *by Tracey Ehman* 69
Wisdom Despite Circumstances *by Dr. Pamela Gunter* 73
Forget Prince Charming *by Helen Hicks* 77
Shine On *by Zan Johns* 81
His Hands and Feet *by Lauren Kirby* 85
Speak Inclusive Words to Hear Inclusive Words *by Paula M. Kramer* 89
Beyond Grief: Rising from Ashes *by Zeenath Kuraisha* 93

Secrets to Success Over Four Decades *by Marsha Lake* 97

Empowered Women Empowering Women *by Gloria Manchester* 101

The Wisdom of Trauma *by Sheliah J. McDaniel*. 105

The Power Within Her Story *by Amber Mesorana*. 109

De-cloaking to Shine My Own Light *by Jennifer Mitchell* 113

I Found My Birth Father *by Fonda Neal* 117

Beyond Belief: How Actions Manifest Miracles *by Kashaun Parker* 121

Laurel's Own Words *by Laurel Anda Charlong Penner*. 125

When Life Throws You Lemons . . . *by Rachel Pietsch*. 129

Journey to Self: Unveiling My Authentic Identity *by Valerie Priester*. 133

Never Waste a Crisis *by Meng Quah-Shepherd*. 137

Breaking the Chains: A Tale of Resilience, Rebellion, and Rebirth
by Alexandra X. Quinn. 141

The Art of Work-Life Integration: Lessons from a Mom Entrepreneur
by Laura Reale. 145

Women Leaders with Healing Hands *by Dr. hc Margareth Reed* 149

From Resilience to Radiance *by Laura Rubinstein* 153

Empowered to Rebuild Against All Odds *by Emmagness Ruzvidzo* 157

Finding My Purpose: A Journey to Health and Fulfillment *by Norva Samuel*. 161

Breaking Barriers: A Journey of Resilience and Empowerment in
Real Estate *by Brigitte Stills* 165

How Free Do You Want to Be? *by Andrea Tompkins* 169

Pissed-off CPA on a Mission *by Ngoc T. Tran, CPA* 173

The Power of Yes: Embrace Your Future! *by Dr. Anne Marie R. Youlio*. . . . 177

Turmoil, Tenacity, and Triumph *by Jeanne Zierhoffer* 181

Foreword

Anne-Marie Dekker

The year is 1971. Even if you were not yet born, I am certain you have heard of Helen Reddy's song "I Am Woman Hear Me Roar." Helen was about thirty years old when she wrote those lyrics. It became the anthem of the women's movement. Words that resonated then were *I'm invincible, I am wise,* and *wisdom born out of pain.*

Fast forward forty-two years to 2013 when, at the age of twenty-nine, Katy Perry writes and records the song "Roar." Like Helen Reddy, Katy and the women of today are adamant to be heard.

The words *wisdom* and *roar* were the first words I wrote down when I started to get my thoughts together for this foreword. I had no idea how I was going to use these words. I was only aware that there was a strong pull between these words and the women writers in this book as well as in the previous *Voices of the 21st Century* books.

I confess, for weeks, *wisdom* and *roar* lived lonely lives on that piece of paper until I'd made my yearly trek to an island where our family's cottage is located. It's never an easy trip. It takes about nine hours from door to door to travel. It's just a hundred miles, two ferries, and a long drive between the two ferry terminals—an hour's waiting time, if you're lucky. The next to almost final leg of this journey is catching the water taxi. I'm almost "home" when we reach the island. The final part is the unloading of several Rubbermaid bins onto a "land" taxi, an old but still workable truck. This trip was no different from the previous ones, except a very strong westerly wind was heading toward the small island.

Once at the cottage, I watched the ocean become turbulent, producing white caps on the crescent of each wave. I heard the whistling of the wind. As the waves crashed onto the shore, there was the added deafening sound of stirred-up pebbles. I watched the interaction of the wind, the ocean, and the land, and my mind went to the stories waiting to be told by the women in this book. I thought of the strength of the voices of these women. I thought of their coming through their journeys. Most of all, I thought of their wisdom, their legacy, the roar that came through their fire, and their feeling invincible as the champions they were always meant to be. In my mind, I heard the wonderful voice of Maya Angelou: "People are so much greater than they think they are."

We have so much more in common with each other than we often realize. Your story might not be my story, at least not yet. Not until your stories might give me—or anyone—the transformation needed in times of turbulence.

It took three days for the wind to subside. Just as suddenly as the strong winds had come up, so did the hush of silence. There was a peaceful aura to this silence. It anchored me to a time when I was on holiday in Thailand. I had been observing a young lady with a small basket filled with lotus flowers still in the buds. Oblivious to her surroundings, she began taking out the still-budded flowers, one at a time. She cupped each of them between her hands and, with careful and deft precision, took a petal, folded the tip under, and repeated this action with all the other petals. The final result was a stunning transformation of an already beautiful flower. Instead of letting the bud open up, the flower would stay as a bud.

The lotus flower begins its life as a seed in dirty, muddy water. After germination, a tiny seedling emerges, roots, and starts to grow in the mud. It then grows leaves and a bud. Eventually, the leaves and the flower bud are pushed toward the light above the murky water. Once above the water, the bud opens into a flower for a couple of hours before it closes again and retreats under water. This ritual is repeated for four days when the flower returns back to the mud to become nourishment for the next flower.

The stories we read in *Voices of the 21st Century* are much like the leaves and lotus flowers rising from the mud or the crashing waves. How often have we found ourselves stuck in the mud? How often have we only heard the deafening sound of waves crashing onto the beach, stirring up sand and pebbles?

When we find ourselves in difficult situations, we look for the stillness that follows the turbulence. Or, like the lotus flower, we push ourselves out of the murky water. We look for our *wisdom*. We find our power.

Treasure each story in this book. They and your own story are your *roars*. You are invincible. You are *wise*. You are the champion.

***Anne-Marie Dekker** is a story catcher, storyteller, and narrative coach. She is curious about people and the world. She has created and operated companies in the entertainment, broadcasting, and magazine industries. She presently uses her skills in a new and exciting marketing agency, where Mother Nature is its only client.*

NatureAgency.org

EMBRACING YOUR VOICE: A JOURNEY TO BELIEF

Gail Watson

Growing up, my life was pretty simple but also kind of complicated. I was adopted into a family that immigrated to Canada, looking for a better life. They believed in working hard, really hard, for everything they wanted. My family valued hard work over vocal expression, and I learned early on the importance of diligence and perseverance. It was a humble family, and my dad used to say, "I do the work that Canadians don't want to do."

Some of my relatives didn't quite see me as truly being a part of the family. Hearing "You're not real" from them was tough. Those words, though perhaps not intended to hurt me, etched a narrative of doubt and invisibility into my young mind. It's funny how words like that stick with you, making you doubt yourself and your place in the world. My childhood was marked by silence; I was the quiet, shy girl who preferred the background, believing it was where I belonged. I often felt a lot of pressure to fit in, and I wanted to fit in, not just with them but with the world outside, too.

Learning from my parents the value of hard work, working hard is what I did. My first job was at fourteen years old, and I don't think I've stopped since then! Embodying the role of the worker bee, buzzing from one task to another, and saving my earnings to buy the things I desired, gave me a sense of value. This work ethic, instilled from a young age, became my armor, shielding me from the insecurities whispering doubts in my ear.

However, life has a way of challenging us to step beyond our comfort zones, question the status quo, and dare for more. For me, this turning point came not through a grand epiphany but through a series of small victories and realizations. Despite lacking a post-secondary degree, I found myself competing for—and winning—roles over those who had the formal education I lacked. It was in these moments that a new belief began to take root: perhaps what I had to say and what I could do truly mattered.

This newfound confidence didn't bloom overnight. It was a slow, deliberate process, much like the lotus flower emerging with boldness from murky waters. My professional successes began to influence my personal life, transforming my self-doubt into belief in my own worth and the value of my voice. This transformation was supported by a circle of friends I had made from a youth group I was involved in that became my foundation of trust. Their unwavering support and shared experiences helped me believe in myself, which boosted my confidence, illustrating the profound impact of community and self-belief in realizing one's true potential.

Community makes a difference.

In my conversations with others, I often see my former self: voices dimmed by doubt, questioning their worth and the significance of their message. "I don't have value," they say, or "Why would someone want to listen to me?" It is in these moments that I lean in, fueled by a desire to uplift and empower. I see in them the potential for transformation, for I, too, have walked the path from silence to using my voice.

The journey to find and own your voice is deeply personal. It is our power of belief, not only in ourselves but in the value of our messages. Through the Women Speakers Association, I have had the privilege of witnessing countless women discover this truth for themselves. Each story, each voice, adds a unique part to our collective human experience, reminding us that diversity in thought and expression is not just valuable; it is vital.

My message and the core belief of the Women Speakers Association is simple:

Your message matters.

It is a declaration, a call to action for every woman who has ever doubted her worth or the significance of her voice. We are all born with a gifted message, a unique contribution to the world that can only be made by us. And for this message to have an impact, it must be shared.

There is no message greater and no message less than your gifted message.

The journey to believing in this truth may be fraught with challenges, but it is a path worth traversing. It is not just a journey of self-discovery but of empowerment and liberation.

As you move forward, remember that your voice and your story have the power to inspire, heal, and transform. Embrace your unique message with confidence and courage, for in doing so, you not only illuminate your own path but light the way for others.

Words of wisdom:

Believe in the power of your voice. Your message is a gift to the world, one that deserves to be heard. Embrace it, share it, and watch as it transforms not just your life but the lives of those around you. Remember, there is no greater act of courage than to speak your truth and live authentically. Your voice matters—never forget that.

***Gail Watson**, founder and CEO of Women Speakers Association, has championed the empowerment of women's voices across the globe in over 120 countries since 2011. With a commitment to bridging the gender equity gap, her visionary leadership and passion for connecting individuals shine through her words by creating platforms for women to share their stories and create meaningful connections. Gail is dedicated to empowering women to authentically express and build thriving, prosperous businesses to transform the lives of their clients, companies, communities, and the world.*

WomenSpeakersAssociation.com

WHERE SHALL I DIE?

Karen Anderson

*Dedicated to those who mysteriously lost a loved one—
I saw your pain.*

It's a bizarre question to ask, but in what was possibly the darkest moment of my life to date, I had to ask myself, *Where shall I die?* Let me explain.

I thought I was in a loving, committed relationship. Sure, my life partner had been grumpy lately, but we were about to go on a beach holiday, and I was so excited. Two days before we were due to leave, he came in from the garden in a horrible mood. His anger grew, and the next thing I knew, I was running for my life as he threatened me with a carving knife.

For the next few hours, I sat on our bed crying, unable to make sense of what had happened. Periodically, my abuser would ask me why I wasn't ready to go visit his family. Surely, I had finished crying. But my tears seemed unstoppable.

During these brief conversations, I asked him why he'd threatened me. First, he denied it. Then, he tried to minimize it. He hadn't touched me, he'd said, but from my perspective, that shouldn't matter. Threatening a stranger with a knife is against the law; surely, I was worthy of the same protections in my own home. I felt deeply betrayed, knowing the man I thought I could trust with my life had just threatened to end it.

He then gave me one final excuse: I was spending too much time in the kitchen. I call this moment *The Gift of the Dumb Excuse* because it freed me. It was such a weird, random answer, so I didn't feel any blame for his threatened attack. I quickly understood there wasn't anything I could have done that might have prevented his abuse. His thoughts and actions were totally his own; this was such a gift.

But then, the full impact of the meaning struck me. If what prompted the violent thoughts and actions were completely in his head, how could I see them coming? How would I keep myself safe?

That's when I realized I was in serious trouble. I already felt absolutely numb with shock and incapable of making any decisions, but I needed to make an enormous one immediately: Where shall I die?

Sometimes, there are no good decisions, just the decisions we can live with.

I had been so excited about our beachside holiday I hadn't paid attention. I didn't know the name of the town we were visiting, so I couldn't tell anyone where I would be. My greatest fear was if his violence could be sparked by anything, he could kill me while we were away, dump my body in the bush, and no one, including the police, would know where to start searching for me.

I had seen many people interviewed who had lost loved ones in mysterious circumstances without ever knowing what had happened to them. I superimposed my parents on their images, and I began imagining their heartache, spending the remainder of their lives wondering where I was, what had happened, and why I had disappeared.

Hope told me I had nothing to worry about. It was just a one-off, horrible mistake. Everything would be all right once we'd left on our holiday, but doubt kept creeping in. Could I really take the risk?

My other option was to tell him I wasn't going on the holiday. This would risk his anger and his violence and potentially expose me to harm I might otherwise avoid if I just went along with our original plans. If he flew into another rage and killed me at home, the police would have a starting point for their investigations.

What should I do? How could I possibly anticipate the outcome of something that was completely unimaginable when I'd woken up that morning?

If I did nothing and went along with our original holiday plans, I might sentence my parents to a life of pain and anguish, or nothing could happen. If I changed my plans and stayed at home, I could incite a life-threatening rage that could be avoided if I remained compliant.

I had less than a day to make this important decision, a decision that could significantly harm me or save me, and there was no predicting the outcome in advance.

So, what did I do? I came to terms with the fact there was no good decision. All I could do was choose the decision I could live with.

Lessons learned

Luckily, it all worked out. I refused to go on the holiday. It wasn't an easy conversation—in fact, it was tense—but fortunately, my abuser was still so angry with me that I suspect he thought staying at home and missing the holiday was an appropriate punishment for me.

What you might be surprised to learn is that once this moment was behind me, I never thought about it again. You see, there are so many overwhelming decisions to make when you discover you are living in an abusive relationship. Things like how to stay safe and survive each day. The holiday decision was just one thing, an important first step that was quickly ticked off my To Do List.

However, when I was writing the chapter titled "Am I a Ghost?" in *Voices of the 21st Century: Women Empowered Through Passion and Purpose*, I started thinking about why it took a day or two before my ghost-like feelings began. When I finally remembered, I was shocked that this significant moment was so quickly forgotten in the trauma and stress of trying to escape an abusive relationship. Importantly, the lesson itself was never forgotten, and it became a part of my decision-making DNA.

***Karen Anderson** is a multi-award-winning copywriter who uses her communication skills and lived experience to speak openly about the challenges facing victims of domestic violence. She is also the CEO of the Escape to Better Foundation, a charity providing online resources and guidance to people experiencing intimate partner abuse and violence.*

EscapeToBetter.org

Transforming Pain into Purpose—Find Your Blue Rose

Karen Barno

Growing up in a small town as the youngest of three, I had lived a lot of life by the time I'd graduated high school. I had the privilege of overcoming numerous challenges; it was a privilege because I learned inner strength and a growth mindset.

I struggled with a speech impediment, unable to say R's and S's, which meant teasing from my peers. My parents sent me to weekly speech therapy sessions. One unforgettable day, I arrived late to gym class from speech therapy. My class was outside, and it was in the winter, and I had to run through the parking lot—not sure who thought that was a great idea. My PE teacher told me to catch up with the class, so I took off running, hit black ice, face-planted on the ground, and chipped my four front teeth. Ouch.

I was bullied and abused. Surrounded by chaos, I grew used to the severe teasing and a strong sense of being different. I continued to play small. Join the school play? No, thank you. Go to a sleepover? Nope. Raise my hand when I knew the answer? Absolutely not. I knew I was stuck, yet fiercely independent. Most of my childhood was spent alone in my room, hiding while devising an escape plan.

Suddenly, my life shifted in the most unusual way. One cold, dreary winter day in December, I was sitting outside in a large snow drift, watching the sunset over the neighbor's house. Out of nowhere, a woman dressed in white appeared and sat next to me. She was captivating, with green eyes that drew you in and a smile that radiated safety. She glowed.

She looked at me, took a deep breath, and with a gentle smile, said, "Promise me you will hang in there until you are eighteen. You will never quit on yourself."

I stared at her, mesmerized, sure she could see through me to truly understand who I was. It was as if she saw my soul. Tears began rolling down my face. Shaking my head, I meekly whispered, "Yes."

"If you do that, know you will find your way," she assured me. Then, she rose, took a few steps, and added, "Your gifts will scare you, but embrace them. We will be watching you, my love." For the first time in my life, I had hope.

I knew I was here for a larger purpose and needed a plan. For the GI Bill, I joined the U.S. Air Force as a medic straight out of high school. On that journey, I discovered my ability to help people heal physically and spiritually. I uncovered my gift of intuition, connecting deeply with individuals on their healing journeys. Random people would approach me with questions about their health, future, and themselves, expecting me to have the answers. Often, I did.

Fast forward many years. After divine serendipity, I met a group of women who pioneered a new facet of healthcare called assisted living. They envisioned an association where kindred spirits could connect. By another twist of fate, they appointed me as their CEO. Despite having no experience in leadership, I felt an intuitive pull and said yes. Somehow, I knew this was exactly where I belonged. However, I never anticipated the criticism, rejection, and mean comments that caused me to shrink even more over the years.

Then, by chance, I found a book about blue roses. It explained how creating an actual blue rose is genetically impossible. Thus, blue roses symbolize enlightenment, enchantment, hope, new beginnings, and discovering one's purpose. The book reminded me of Gildawish, my guardian angel, whom I hadn't considered in years. Was it a message from her?

COVID hit senior housing a few years later. I had to step up and guide our members through the most challenging times I have ever witnessed. I started doing videos to provide information and policy changes. Then, I embraced public speaking and grew comfortable as a public face. Spending two years alone in our office gave me the time to reflect deeply, helping me understand who I had become and why I was there.

I was being pushed in a direction I didn't fully understand. I put my trust in the Universe and said, "Let's go. I'm ready." I started to notice friends and strangers calling me about work-related topics. The conversations often turned to their challenges: divorce, job issues, or other problems. They sought my advice, convinced I could help, though I didn't share their confidence at the time.

In 2021, I had another profound shift. While driving home from a wedding shower, a storm was fast approaching. In the desert, you can see the storm coming toward you and the sunny sky visible behind it. The rain was so heavy I decided to wait out the storm. Forty-five minutes later, the sun emerged, and something had shifted. I felt a calmness I hadn't experienced in years. My confidence and mojo were back.

I'd found my blue rose. I knew what Gildawish was trying to tell me. I'd rediscovered my purpose.

Each person has a blue rose. Some find it young, while it remains hidden for others, waiting to be discovered amidst their struggles. Your guardian angel will guide you if you follow the signs. They don't all make a physical appearance. Often, they reveal themselves through books, odd comments you overhear, or messages placed within pages.

Rest assured: each woman has a unique calling.

If you heed the whispers carried on the wind, perhaps in the realm of your dreams or while sitting in a snow-laden drift, you will find your blue rose.

This is dedicated to every woman on the quest for her blue rose. Embrace your journey and never lose sight of the greatness within you. Your brilliance is boundless, and your potential is limitless. Keep believing, keep striving, and let your inner light shine.

Karen Barno *is CEO of the advocacy organization AZALFA. She guides women to reclaim their power and heal from past traumas. As a messenger of transformation, Karen helps women uncover their true selves and live their best lives through her Blue Rose Framework.*

KarenBarno.com

Conquering the Silent Saboteur of Imposter Syndrome

Shelly L. Bell

This chapter is dedicated to everybody who has ever felt like an imposter in their own lives. May you have the strength to recognize your worth and confidently accept your successes.

Imagine yourself standing on the precipice of your dreams, the pinnacle of your success within reach. However, an unseen force pulls you back, whispering poisonous doubts in your ear: "You don't belong here." "You're a fraud, and it's only a matter of time before they all find out." Imposter syndrome, a quiet saboteur, may affect even the most accomplished individuals.

What if I told you your inner critic isn't the final arbiter of your worth? What if you could silence that voice and walk boldly into the light of your whole potential? In this chapter, we'll go on a journey to understand and overcome impostor syndrome, turning those debilitating whispers into a loud roar of confidence and strength. Prepare to shake off the shackles of self-doubt and regain your rightful place in the world—your triumph over imposter syndrome begins here.

Imposter syndrome is the feeling of not deserving the praise and recognition you receive despite your achievements. I know first-hand what that feels like because I doubted my skills, talents, and abilities.

Having had the honor and chance to serve in the government, the non-profit sector, and academia, I had the intrinsic capacity to never internalize my accomplishments and always feel as if I did not belong at the table. This was my greatest challenge during my time in academia.

Why? I began my career in admissions as an enrollment counselor before being elevated to special assistant to the president, where I served on the President's Cabinet. I was so consumed by fear and what others thought of me that I worried about being exposed as a fraud.

What is impostor syndrome? It's a companion who questions your talents. It tricks you into believing your accomplishments are only surface-level successes, ready to crumble when scrutinized. When imposter syndrome occurs, you can feel stuck and confined.

The voice in my head, as well as my self-doubt, were continual reminders that I might fall and fail. Most importantly, I wasn't good enough, and I might be discovered. When working on a project with a team, I never felt as if I'd brought value or made a significant contribution. Not to mention the numerous instances in which I was neglected and felt invisible when my team was recognized. Some people have told me they are uncomfortable accepting praise since their brains were trained not to think highly of themselves. I strongly believe this filthy thinking is learned behavior.

When you grow up in a household, you are told to be quiet. At work, you are not supposed to shine or monopolize the spotlight. Oh, and don't get me started about serving in ministry, especially as a woman. If you're confident and know you're competent, there are times when you're naturally neglected, ostracized, denied opportunities, and rendered invisible; when you're confident, you own your achievements and celebrate yourself.

I've realized that some people suffer from insecurity and deliberately make you fail by instilling self-doubt. Unfortunately, I had to take a close look at those I spent time with and recognize that I'd surrounded myself with people who had a significant impact on my development. When you associate with a stagnant circle of underachievers, you might perpetuate a self-limiting mindset. I'm reminded of a scripture in the Bible found in Proverbs 13:20, which says, "We should walk with the wise to gain wisdom." Seek mentors and people who will encourage you to strive for more.

Here's the thing: much of my success is attributable to hard work and a growth mindset. I've invested in myself by returning to school to get an executive master of public administration degree from Rutgers University and a Rutgers certified public managers (CPM) certification. I owe it to myself to celebrate my achievements. It is not about playing small. It is about clapping myself on the back and saying, "You go, girl."

Too frequently, people hold back and let chances pass them by, concerned about what others might say and questioning their ability. There will always be the risk of failure, but you will grow by tackling these fears and stepping outside of your comfort zone. Don't let your anxieties and fears keep you back. Stop wasting energy attempting to prove your worth to others. The irony is you are the only one who believes you are incapable. The only person you have to prove anything to is yourself.

So, how did I overcome the silent saboteur of imposter syndrome? I stopped comparing myself to others. I realized, acknowledged, and accepted that I am unique and different. I stopped feeling inferior and doubting myself because I realized the reality: there will always be someone more beautiful, witty, talented, or intellectual than me.

Stop comparing yourself to others, and instead, look to see if you're fulfilling your full potential and celebrating your achievements. You are more capable than you realize, and if you stop questioning yourself, you can and will accomplish amazing things. What matters most is not whether you are frightened of failing, appear naïve, or not enough; it is whether you allow those fears to keep you from taking the measures needed to achieve your goals.

Finally, to overcome the silent saboteur of imposter syndrome, you must identify and combat negative beliefs that damage your self-esteem, replacing them with affirmations of your genuine abilities and accepting your well-deserved accomplishments.

Moving forward, I will keep in mind that my worth is defined by the strength of my own belief in my talents rather than external validation. Corinthians 5:17 says, "Therefore, if anyone is in Christ, the new creation has come: the old has gone, the new is here!" This is a reminder that my value comes from being a new creation in Christ, not from my achievements or others' opinions.

Shelly L. Bell *is an encourager with her infectious smile, commanding demeanor and voice, and a motivator. In addition to being the principal and founder of Shelly Speaks, LLC, she is a bestselling author, professional emcee, and inspirational speaker. Her presentations are remarkable, combining humor, humility, and honesty to inspire her audience to take action and reach their full potential.*

ShellyLBell.com

Raising Voices and Raising Capital

Victoria Bennett

My son, James, was four years old when his junior kindergarten teacher recommended he join the Calgary Boys' Choir. We'd never heard of the group, but it was a well-established set of choirs that sang increasingly complex music, some very traditional, some very modern, but constantly engaging for boys who liked to be seen and heard. James enjoyed playing soccer, but the choir was his other team sport. Over the years, I got more involved and was invited onto the board, probably because I liked being engaged, because I was a little vocal, and because of my marketing skill set.

It was approaching the choir's fortieth anniversary. While this was an important milestone for the choir, it was not necessarily the most engaging for the boys. I recommended we rename it the "40th Birthday," something the boys could relate to. In the same board meeting, I heard about Calgary becoming the "City of Culture" and that a crowdfunding platform was being created to fund different art projects in the city. The board chair asked me to run a crowdfunding campaign for the choir's fortieth birthday.

I asked what crowdfunding was, and they said they would introduce me to someone who would explain. That was where my crowdfunding journey started. I soon understood that crowdfunding is raising a large amount of money from small amounts given by people in your "crowd," or in this case, the Calgary Boys' Choir community. We contacted the current boys, their families, the alumni, and the arts community in Calgary at large. We let people know what we were crowdfunding for and what the impact of their backing the campaign would be. We thanked everyone who backed the birthday crowdfund and asked them to share it with their networks.

I also learned much more. This campaign was a rewards campaign where people got something back, unlike a donations campaign where you give to a cause. In this case, backers received CDs from the choir plus offers of performances, depending on the amount backed. You might be familiar with Kickstarter or Indiegogo, where you can get early access to new things or an experience not available anywhere else. There are also more business-focused crowdfunding, peer-to-peer lending, royalties (think *Dragon's Den*), and equity.

I started to get really excited. A team, including my husband and I, had set up an oil and gas service company. We put in sweat equity to start it up and real dollars to help it grow. Believing in something and meeting an unmet market need was close to mind. With equity crowdfunding, it wasn't just a small group of people who could back something they believed in; it was everyone across the country.

This gave me much greater access to capital and would validate any business idea. I started researching. Brewing was a big crowdfunding topic at the time. Brewdog had just started in the UK, and they were getting people to back their beer and grow their company. Being able to go out for a drink with friends and say, "I own the company," was a game-changer.

I also realized there was another side to this story. It was not just the companies that gained access to capital, but the investors gained access to companies and to investments they would typically not have as they weren't directly related to the business or weren't already super-wealthy. Early-stage companies have the highest risk but also the highest reward. Think of Google, Apple, and all of the other guys who started in a garage. The reality is that very few companies make the unicorn status of being that $1 billion company, but they may go from $0 to a few million.

When I realized the two-sided nature of the democratization of capital, I got really excited. By that time, we'd sold our company, and I knew my husband would travel much more. I also knew I needed more flexibility with our two little people, so I decided to go into consulting: strategic marketing, of course, but also crowdfunding. There was no one else helping people crowdfund in Canada, and by that time, with all my research, I had a pretty good understanding of the process.

It has been an exciting ride. Now, ten years on, I have grown from a company of one to a company of six. We have supported over one hundred crowdfunding campaigns and raised over $20 million. I like that we are helping purpose-led businesses, ones that are making an impact and ones you can tell a story about, from the pain-free needle for insulin injections to vertical farming for a plant-based protein company that could provide high-quality food close to where people live, including areas where it is nearly impossible to grow food.

It's not always plain sailing. Over the years, we have developed our own processes and systems. The world is constantly changing, and what worked last year, even last month, may not work this month. Plus, companies also need to be really honest with themselves: do they really have something better, faster, and cheaper than what is already out there and in a growing marketplace? I have had to be the one telling people their business is a hobby or that they should focus on the problem rather than the solution, but this is the experience working with start-ups and growth companies over the past ten years and the crowdfunding campaign eleven years ago has given me. I remember wondering why I had been given the project to run the campaign for the Calgary Boys' Choir. Now, I am so grateful to have been a part of something so dynamic that has given me many opportunities to make an impact.

Victoria Bennett *hails from the UK, where she studied biochemistry, used her science as a steppingstone into technical brand management on Ariel/Tide, and honed her marketing skills with Pampers and TD Bank. She is a strategic marketer and an ardent crowdfunding supporter, coach, consultant, speaker, and now author.*

TheCrowdfundingHub.com

MORE THAN ENOUGH

Dr. Renae Bjorg

Recently, God gave me a vision of how I was created.

Before the beginning of time, God called me. "Renae! Renae! Come here. I want to show you something," exclaimed God.

"What is it, God?" I squealed with childlike wonder.

"I have an idea. I am going to create this place called Earth. It will be magnificent. What do you think?"

I jumped up and down with glee.

"Do you want to go there?" God queried.

"Yes! Yes!" I raised my hand. "Pick me!"

God said, "You already have everything you need for planet Earth, but I want to give you more." With that, he reached up, pinched the air, and deposited an unseen substance in me. He laughed and clapped his hands, and I knew he was creating his masterpiece: me. Again and again, he pinched the air and deposited something in me, and each time, he seemed more elated than the last. He burst with happiness and pride. He was delighted in ME, his creation. I could not see the invisible substance, but I experienced being made *in* Love, *with* Love, and *by* Love. I was born out of the goodness of God.

And then I came to Earth. I was the second-born in a family of eight children. We lived in the heart of the Red River Valley, where the soil was rich and the crops were abundant. In those long days of summer, I went on walks with God. We held hands as we sojourned through the woods, around the lake, or under the stars. Sometimes, I asked him a question or expressed an idea, and he would ask, "What do you think about that, Renae?" In God's eyes, what I had to say was important. I was significant.

Then, an event happened that caused fear to take root. I distrusted myself and others. In fact, I became terrified of people and dimmed my light until I became invisible. I felt disconnected from my own life force. I cried out to God, "What is wrong with me?"

God said, "You always get the answers to the questions you ask. Ask me a different question." Confused, I asked for clarity. God said, "If you believe there is something wrong with you, you will always find something wrong with you."

That simple statement changed my life. My perception shifted, and I began to see unlimited possibilities. Then, God gave me a vision for healing.

It was in a sacred space of healing. In the center of the room was a table, much like one you would find in a clinic. Just beneath the tabletop was a drawer. A patient was lying on the table, and I was standing beside it, simply loving him. A moment or two passed, and I opened the drawer. The cancer that was in the patient had fallen out of him and into the drawer. "What? God, the cancer fell out of him!" I removed the drawer and marveled at how easy it was for cancer to fall out of people before it was flushed down the toilet. Another patient, and then another, and another received healing, and then something incredible happened. I was carrying the drawer with the cancer in it to the toilet, and it suddenly disappeared. "God, what is this? Where did the cancer go?" I questioned. God showed me the thoughts of the person on the table: "My children never paid attention to me until I got cancer. If I don't have cancer, I will never see them again." With that thought, she took the cancer back. A second patient took back the cancer when he thought, "I am on disability. If I do not have cancer, I cannot claim benefits."

It was incredulous to me that there was a payoff for illness until I had my own brush with cancer.

A routine mammogram picked up something "suspicious." After a second mammogram, an ultrasound, and a biopsy, I was diagnosed with invasive ductal carcinoma in the right breast. The surgeon gave me four protocols for treatment: surgery, radiation, chemotherapy, and hormone blockers. He advised that I have surgery immediately and seemed dumbfounded when I did not choose any of his recommendations.

Instead, I asked God, "What is it going to take for me to let go of cancer?" and he responded, "Love yourself."

It was easy for me to love others, but not as easy to love myself. Through the course of a year, I learned that working on loving myself was not the same as *actually* loving myself. I had to rewrite my story to love and accept myself. "What is it going to take to love myself?" I asked. This time, instead of focusing on the how and the doing, I focused on allowing and being.

I was lying on my bed, and my Infinite Self stood beside me. She was radiant, and I was mesmerized by her exquisite beauty. In fact, she was beauty itself poured out . . . a masterpiece. The same masterpiece that had stood with God before the beginning of time. She was God's delight.

It was as though I was suddenly back in the healing room. This time, I was the patient lying on the table, and my Infinite Self was the me standing beside the table. At first, when she reached her hand to mine, I was terrified. The words, "I am unworthy to receive you," popped into my head. I asked, "What is it going to take to be worthy to receive you, Renae?" The unworthiness immediately left my body and was gone. This time, when she reached for my hand, we embraced. At that moment, my heart expanded, and the dim light we once were became one giant, expansive beam. I became the Renae who God delighted in creating before the beginning of time.

You are a powerful, creative genius . . . a masterpiece. If you feel disconnected from your own brilliance, simply change your question. The universe always delivers exactly what you ask for.

***Dr. Renae Bjorg** delightfully lights the path for all those who have not yet answered the call of their souls. Her passion is to help women awaken to their true nature and expand their consciousness. She empowers them to embrace and experience their exquisite beauty through love and creative self-expression.*

IAmRenae.com

CARING FOR KYRA

Glendoria Phillips Boyd

My husband and I were married when he was sixty-three and I was sixty-two—no spring chickens. We were married three years—still newlyweds—when Kyra, my husband's niece, joined us. I'd always assumed newlyweds would spend at least the first five years alone before people moved in or trouble came, but after only three years of wedded bliss, here came Kyra.

Kyra was no ordinary person. She had Huntington's disease. My husband hadn't explained that this progressive disease was in his family line. I'd known my husband from way back when we were still young and in lust. He'd confessed that he had a daughter, so I imagined they were a "normal" family. Not so. They had a generational illness called Huntington's, a crippling disease that only got worse, and there was no cure.

I remember when Kyra arrived. She could still walk and talk but couldn't use her hands. I wanted to be a good wife by helping her out, yet I hated every minute of it. I remember thinking in my youth that I would never do any caregiving! It was the pit of all jobs. I preferred working all day in the sun to being a caregiver because the patients were seniors, senile, and incontinent. No way! But Kyra was young and intelligent. She needed help. Still, I hated the fact that I was the chosen helper.

I can honestly say that if it had not been for the Lord on my side, I don't know where I would be. I was a stay-at-home wife, not a caregiver! I have never been a fan of the sick and/or shut-in. I never wanted to be a nurse. I wanted to work in an office as a secretary of some sort and dress cute. If people were different from me physically or mentally, then I wanted nothing to do with them. My carnal mind had me convinced they were imperfect. All my life, I had wanted nothing to do with deformities of any kind. The thought of it made my flesh crawl. I guess one could say I was sort of like the Pharisees and Sadducees of the New Testament. In my finite thinking, I figured these people were cursed by God.

But God spoke to me in Cap Haitian, Haiti, in 2017, when He put me right smack into the middle of a Haitian city full of all kinds of infirmities. I had to adjust because I was there for nine days, whether I liked it or not. My eyes were opened up to a whole new way of life, and it was not pleasant. I was suddenly up close and personal, especially with the babies and little children. I recall the moment my husband picked up one of those babies and put it on my lap. No! I did not instantly fall in love. I almost freaked out. All I could see was my limbs falling off. I asked God for the strength to not take off running. I had to adjust to holding these children, touching them, looking into their little eyes, and seeing the love of God. I had to embrace them. I would return to the mission home at night and shower until I felt as if my insides were clean, but the Lord spoke to me, reminding me that I could not wash off my negative feelings or stinking thinking because it was deeply rooted inside of me. I realized I was engaged in spiritual warfare. I had to let go of my negative feelings and let God rebuild me from the inside out. I needed healing from God.

God changed my circumstances by letting me get married after forty years of being single. I believe this was God's strategic move to get me to where I am today, helping others. I believe that God saw something in me I did not see in myself. Yes, He gave me that husband I'd prayed for, but with it came his disabled niece. Not only had God orchestrated my marriage but my life, and He gave me a vocation I swore I would never do.

God healed me. I'd had a "disability" of mind and purpose. It wasn't anything I had done well before, but maybe because of my niece's prayers and praises, God had chosen me to take care of her. It wasn't because I wanted to but because He wanted me to. It was an honor to have been chosen by God. Not only did He arrange my present circumstances, but He equipped me for the task. When people see my niece praising God on Sunday, they wonder why she is praising Him. What does she have to praise Him for? Then I think to myself that maybe she is praising Him for me. Yes, for me, because I am the one God chose to take GOOD care of her, and I do it for Him!

I noticed that the more I fought against taking care of her, the harder the job became. Being a Christian, I experienced a lot of guilt.

Some days, I screamed, ran away from home, cried, pitied myself, and whined, but I did the work. I endured the God-forsaken job for my newly-acquired niece. My Christlike spirit ministered to me through God's word. I realized I wasn't being used by my husband but by God. I was being strengthened in Christlikeness. I worked in the spirit of God and demonstrated the fruit of the spirit of Jesus Christ. I learned to act out my teachings because I love God.

Today, I work in a spirit of love and gentleness, caring for Kyra plus two other clients I enjoy to the utmost. Being wise is demonstrating the God-given abilities we possess in Christ Jesus and using those talents and abilities to glorify Him.

Glendoria Phillips Boyd *is a minister of God's word, poet, bestselling author, and motivational speaker. A graduate of Dallas Bible Theology Institute, she holds a Master Certificate from the Childrend's Ministry Institute. She is a member of Gamma Phi Delta Sorority, Inc., and a branch councilor for Foresters Financial Insurance.*

WritingsOfWisdom.com

Believing in the Transformational Power of Virtues

Florine Clomegah-Freitas

My father passed away about a year ago. Throughout my life, he instilled in me the wisdom of Rabelais, paraphrasing it as, "Do everything you want, as long as it is virtuous," or "Do what pleases you so long as it is good." In my twenties, convinced of the transformative power of virtues, I embarked on a quest for truth, encouraged by my late father. After reading a chapter titled "Never Abandon the Path of Virtues," I made a solemn vow in my mid to late twenties never to stray from this path. Raised in the ethos of the Abbey of Thelema by my father, I was immersed in a utopian world where virtues such as honor, integrity, generosity, intellectual curiosity, and freedom formed the cornerstone of our existence. I pledged never to forsake such a world.

In his book, Rabelais elaborates on virtues, including purity, honesty, generosity, courage, wisdom, humility, friendship, joyfulness, resilience, and curiosity.

Unveiling the essence of virtue—a multicultural exploration: Virtues, stemming from the Latin word *virtus*, meaning strength and courage, are essential in nurturing goodness and guiding moral conduct across diverse cultures. Ancient Egypt revered Maat, symbolizing truth and order, while modern African societies cherish Ubuntu, emphasizing community and mutual caring.

Ancient Greek philosophers like Aristotle and Plato laid foundational frameworks for virtues such as wisdom and justice that have influenced European and American values centered around dignity, freedom, and community. Similarly, virtues in South and Central American cultures strongly emphasize family unity and respect.

In Western societies, Christian values like faith, hope, love, and forgiveness profoundly impact personal morality and global ethical standards. Meanwhile, Middle Eastern, Muslim, and Arab cultures value compassion and patience, enhancing social bonds and community resilience. These societies also highly regard hospitality and justice, reflecting a commitment to fairness and altruism.

Japanese culture holds harmony, respect, and politeness in high regard, which is vital for maintaining social order and personal honor. *Gaman*—diligence and perseverance under adversity—is a celebrated virtue. Chinese culture emphasizes harmony, filial piety, and loyalty, driven by Confucian ethics that influence moral conduct and interpersonal relationships.

Buddhist and Hindu traditions prioritize compassion and wisdom respectively, guiding personal actions and societal interactions. Mindfulness and an understanding of life's impermanence underpin ethical living in Buddhist practice, while Hinduism stresses *dharma*, or moral duty, promoting righteous living and societal harmony.

Jewish and Israeli virtues like *tzedakah* (charity) and *chesed* (kindness) emphasize social justice and compassionate acts. *Tikkun olam* (repairing the world) and lifelong Torah study also play significant roles in these cultures.

The Pacific Indigenous cultures' practices of *Aloha* and *Mana* focus on love and nature's interconnectedness. Australia and New Zealand prioritize inclusivity and environmental stewardship.

Embracing this diversity of virtues fosters a more inclusive understanding of morality, inspiring a commitment to goodness and moral excellence globally, underscoring the universal importance of virtues in creating a harmonious and inclusive world.

Key virtues common to humanity: These include compassion, empathy, kindness, integrity, and resilience. These virtues transcend cultural, geographical, and societal boundaries, serving as fundamental principles that promote harmony, understanding, and mutual respect among all individuals.

Practice makes perfect: Having experienced the transformative power of practicing virtues firsthand, I strongly encourage others to engage in this journey for self-improvement. Once consumed by fear, I now understand that boldness and fearlessness are not just qualities but a form of genius in navigating life's challenges. Finding and using my voice required immense courage, but it has been immensely rewarding. Learning to listen to the voice of one's heart and speak one's truth with authenticity is crucial. Virtues help us lead from the heart and discover the interconnectedness of body, heart, mind, intellect, and soul.

SWOT and PESTLE frameworks: Conducting a SWOT analysis enables individuals to identify strengths, weaknesses, opportunities, and threats, initiating their spiritual, human, and social development. Furthermore, considering the political, economic, social, technological, legal, and environmental contexts through a PESTLE analysis helps in comprehending external influences on character. These frameworks guide individuals in prioritizing virtues aligned with their principles, values, and aspirations.

The transformation: The importance of committing to a virtuous life for personal growth and fulfillment cannot be overstated. Through practices such as serenity, control of the senses, resilience, and discerning faith, individuals can align themselves with their purpose and overcome obstacles on their journeys. The pursuit of virtue is not merely a moral obligation but a transformative process that leads to inner peace, stability, and alignment with one's life purpose.

Throughout my years as a truth-seeker, studying under the guidance of the world's best teachers, mentors, and coaches, I have come to deeply understand the importance of embracing the path of virtue as the very essence of wisdom and the gateway to spiritual liberation. The pinnacle of self-realization or self-actualization is a state of inner happiness and perfection that resides within each individual, and this transformative journey is facilitated by the cultivation of virtue. Virtue transcends mere moral duty; it is a science, a potent force that purges unspiritual impressions from the mind and propels consciousness toward the sublime. There is an imperative to embrace virtue without delay; it is akin to a life-saving opportunity that must not be squandered. The pursuit of virtue is integral to both personal and spiritual evolution, serving as the cornerstone of one's peace, bliss, and ultimate freedom. By committing to the daily, unwavering practice of virtue, one can truly become the finest version of oneself.

Therefore, I urge you to tread the path of virtue steadfastly, for it leads to the highest echelons of happiness and wisdom. It all begins with a single step: believing in the power of virtue.

***Florine Clomegah-Freitas** is an alumna of the University Panthéon-Sorbonne, SOAS, Civil Service College, and HEC. A humanitarian director, coach, consultant, SME co-chairwoman, and corporate trainer, she helps others unlock their potential. Passionate about alleviating suffering, she dedicates her writing to empowering transformative change and creating positive life shifts.*

WorldwideWomenForum.org

The Mephibosheth Syndrome: Restoration is Available and Comes from God

Karen L. Collins

What time I am afraid, I will trust in Thee. Psalm 56:3 (KJV)

Wanting to become better equipped to teach children about God's love and share my wisdom and vision of God's plan for my life, I embarked on a journey I was destined to meet sooner or later. I enrolled in the Children's Ministry Institute's (CMI) Instructor of Teachers (IOT1) class three months after my 2018 mandatory retirement as a federal officer. The IOT1 class was designed to enhance my training and passion by equipping other teachers to minister effectively to children.

At the age of fifty-seven, I knew God had more in store for me. I asked Him to put me into full-time ministry. Little did I know I was about to encounter God on another level and face my five-year-old self at the same time.

The purpose God had in store for me would propel me into a long overdue birthing season, I quickly learned. It was the feeling I believe Sarah had when she gave birth to Isaac (see Genesis 21). I had been waiting in the wings to become a published author, and at the age of sixty-three, I gave birth to the purpose only God could provide me with.

I switched gears to learn how to teach adults instead of children in IOT1. I was quite comfortable teaching children, but to teach adults what I knew? Now, that was a different ball game.

Reflecting on that time, I realize my journey was partly shaped by one event occurring in 1966. That's when I ran into Mephibosheth's story. He was the grandson of Saul, the first king of Israel, and the son of Jonathan, who was best friends with David. Mephibosheth was heir to the throne after his father. However, a battle ensued between David's and Saul's armies, and Saul and Jonathan were killed on the same day.

Mephibosheth's nurse found out that Saul and Jonathan had died in the battle, so she picked Mephibosheth up and started running with him to hide him from potential and probable execution. In their escape, the nurse dropped him, crippling Mephibosheth for the rest of his life.

During the IOT1 class, I spent time thinking about the correlation between Mephibosheth's story and mine. I recalled that when I was five, my world had come crashing down on me.

What happened? All I understand and remember is that my friend was in heaven and with Jesus. Years later, I found out that she, her father, and her siblings were in a boat, and it somehow tipped over. She and two of her siblings had drowned in the lake.

After my friend's death, I became pensive and began to overeat. I developed a speech problem and was placed in speech therapy.

My friend's death led me to dive deep into the Bible to ensure my entrance into heaven. Thus, I am passionate about teaching children about Jesus, His resurrection, and His restoring power.

Another connection I have with Mephibosheth's story occurred when King David restored Mephibosheth and gave him his father's inheritance, and David told Mephibosheth that he would eat at the king's table for the rest of his life! After I trusted Jesus as my Savior, I was welcomed into God's house and seated at His table forever.

At the end of class, in obedience to God, I stood before my classmates and told them about the Mephibosheth within me. I felt God restoring my crippled self. Here's my battle cry:

> This birthing process ignites
> The passionate delight
> Of what the Lord can do.
>
> Don't waste your time
> Just keep in line
> Of the pace God will set for you.

And when the battle is done
We will meet The Son
The past will be no issue.

Just stay in the faith
That leads to God's grace
My God, He'll see you through.

Karen L. Collins *is a retired federal probation officer, teacher, and missionary. She is the author of* Where's That Probation Officer?!, Beyond the Clouds, *and* Juneteenth, What Do You Think? *Karen has a master's degree in Family Studies, a bachelor's degree in Criminal Justice, and a Master Teacher certificate from the Children's Ministry Institute.*

KC-DrewsomeWritersLLC.com

The Power of Starting Over

Tracy Conway

To Melody Wonder:
May the light of your love and wisdom continuously
overflow the hearts of all you embraced.

A few years ago, I heard a presentation on generational curses. I had never heard this term before, but when the presenter spoke on how families pass down patterns, beliefs, and ideologies, I thought, "Yes, I can see where this might have happened in my family." I recognized how I had already repeated and broken away from the pattern. Today, I am happily married and have a blended family with five wonderful children: three by birth and two bonus children. I have an amazing career that has allowed me to thrive while finding a love for service and bettering others as I look forward to what the future holds.

I was not always this woman. Twelve years ago, I was in a quite different place mentally, emotionally, and physically. The path to get to where I am is nothing short of God's grace and my own willpower. Let me tell you about starting over. In 2012, I learned I was pregnant with my youngest son. This was crushing news at the time because I was already a single mom of two. I was sleeping on my sister's couch and in an unhealthy relationship. Having an abortion the year prior was one of my biggest regrets; therefore, having my baby was the only option. As my belly began to grow, and after several failed job interviews, I decided to go to school to obtain certifications that would open doors of opportunity. Over the next year, I managed to complete the requirements for my certifications; it was not easy. The people with whom I chose to keep company, my romantic relationship, and my living arrangements went through simultaneous turmoil, causing me to question my capability as a woman, a mother, a partner, and my being as a whole.

In the early part of 2013, I made the decision to move my family, myself, my partner, and our three children into a shelter. I realize today that this was the first phase of starting over. I began searching for employment that aligned with the certificate I'd acquired in school. Of course, every employer wanted experience. As a result, I did odd jobs because I knew that I would not remain where I was forever. Throughout the entire ordeal, my relationship with my partner continued to spiral downward, and in September 2013, we decided to part ways. After the break-up, I did not have secure employment or a vehicle to drive. Ending an almost ten-year relationship with the one person who was supporting us financially put a major hole in my pockets. I thought to myself, "You must be bat crazy—how are you going to take care of these kids and yourself? You have nothing!" Nevertheless, I knew I'd made the right decision because the relationship was unhealthy, not only for me but for him, and especially for my children.

I had grown up in an environment where arguing, yelling, cursing, and fighting were the norms, not just in my home but also in my community. Although I had vowed NEVER to succumb to that environment, I had done just that. I'd exposed my children to the very behaviors that had caused me anxiety, sadness, and pain. I knew that was not fair, and it had gone on long enough. My children had not asked to be in this world, and as their momma, it was up to me to make some changes. Of course, this decision came with many, many nights of crying myself to sleep, thinking, "How did I get here?" I experienced self-loathing and even a pity party at times. I would then think, "Well, Tracy, what did you do that caused you to end up in this space, and how do you fix it?" but there were no answers in sight. One evening, as I lay in my room, crying and having a pity party, my friends gathered in the shared area to watch the music awards. Tamale Mann was performing "Take Me to the King." On a normal evening, I would not have heard the TV as the kids would have been yelling and playing outside of my room, but on that night, I heard the TV. It was so clear as if it were right next to me. At that moment, I knew I was in God's hands.

The next week, I received a call from an agency asking me to come in for an interview. I was so sick that day; however, I had to get my life together to get to the interview. I took some medication, borrowed a shirt from a friend, headed to the interview, and prayed my belly would not make any sounds. Not only did I get the job, but I would also be paid more than I had originally asked for. Over the next ten months, my uncle gave me a car, I was able to save some money, I started dating my now-husband, and I moved out of the facility (which is what we called the shelter). Over the past ten years, I have been blessed with a wonderful marriage, grown in an amazing career doing what brings me joy and peace, and purchased a home. I have gone to therapy to continue building my ability to cope with past feelings and memories as they arise because I have learned they WILL arise. However, I am most grateful for the ability to have an impact on my children, and hopefully their children, by shifting the patterns, behaviors, and ideologies of my family.

My oldest son said to me one day, "Mom, I am proud of you. You have done all the things you said you would do." From that moment, I knew The Power of Starting Over.

I leave my reader with this:

If it seems impossible and painful, START OVER!

If it feels uncomfortable and unbearable, START OVER!

If you are scared and do not know how, START OVER!

The power is in YOU, so START OVER ANYWAY!

***Tracy Conway** is a community advocate who promotes the importance of community engagement, improving health outcomes and overall mental and physical well-being. She is the CEO of Women ICU, a non-profit designed to empower women to excel in their purpose by embracing their past.*

Conway.Tracy@outlook.com

Someone once Told Me that I Could Not Change The World, and for Far Too Long, I Believed Them

TC Cooper

When writing essays, I begin with the question: what do I want the reader to take away from this piece? I write with that end in mind. I hope this essay inspires you to be your most creative self and amplify your voice to positively impact every person and situation you encounter.

Here's what I know: You were born a creative person, and your creativity lives in your voice. Your voice uniquely reflects your hopes, dreams, lived experiences, values, and wisdom. When activated, your voice impacts not only the people who directly interact with you but also the world around them. Every person who listens to your words, reads them, or is inspired by your artistic expression has a sphere of influence that becomes shaped by your voice. **This essay is my love letter to you.**

As an executive coach, personal brand strategist, and corporate attorney educated at some of the world's best schools, you might assume that recognizing the power of my creative voice and valuable contributions to my industries would come naturally to me. *If you assumed this, you assumed wrong.*

For as long as I can remember, a creative voice has lived inside me, urging me to live outside what was expected of me. This has been true in high school, college, law school, and even while practicing law and running my businesses. Yet I often stayed just within the edge of my comfort zone. **I believed the lie that I couldn't change the world, so I stayed in my little box of comfort, doing enough to have an impact but not to make a measurable difference.**

This may sound familiar to you. Believing the lie that you can't change the world and then playing yourself small by not trying. And then, instead of using your God-given talents to do what you can to effect change, you fall into a pattern of being safe—playing around the edges of your passions, careful not to do "too much" to avoid criticism, or worse, rejection. I know this way of being, and I lived there for entirely too long, not breaking out until I made the decision to BE BOLD. **Too many leaders lose their creative voices by trying to be someone they're not, leaving the world poorer for it.**

For those of us who followed a traditional, linear path to what we believed was success—high school, college, graduate school, a good job, marriage, and so forth—this is especially true. While this path is honorable, it is not the only measure of success, and it's easy to lose yourself and give away your creative voice when trying to make this vision your reality.

Many high-achieving professionals have a creative voice hidden deep inside, yearning for attention and care, a voice that whispers of untapped potential and dreams yet to be realized. Being a wise human means nurturing, caring for, and cultivating this creative voice for your greatest good and the good of those around you.

Here's what I've learned along my ever-evolving journey to become a wiser woman: **wisdom knows that if you don't use your voice to accomplish the work you've been created to do, it won't be done in the unique way you are called to do it.** Too often, people—especially women—hide their voices out of fear of rejection and disapproval. Through my experiences and those of my clients, I've seen that suppressing our creative voices can look like avoiding conflict by ignoring microaggressions, missing opportunities to lead by example, walking away from relationships instead of working through differences, staying in a career that no longer supports who you are called to be because you are worried about what people think, or hiding in your career under the illusion that you have plenty of time to activate your dreams. *You have less time than you think but enough to start now.*

Sound familiar?

When you activate your voice and cultivate its creativity, acts of suppression can be transformed into opportunities for growth and wisdom. **Your voice, when cultivated, inspires creativity in all areas of life, both personal and professional.**

The first step in cultivating your most creative voice is to connect and reconnect with yourself by focusing on your well-being—spiritual, mental, and physical. I developed a framework that has been essential to my clients and me as we cultivate and breathe life into our creative voices. It's called BE BOLD.

There are a number of ways you can integrate BE BOLD into your life. Believe in your unique voice and its power. Cultivate and care for the creative voice within you, the one that goes against the grain and leads you to your passions. **Embrace** your creativity without fear or hesitation. Trust that God has placed the desires of your heart in your heart for a reason and a season. **Build** a supportive environment and surround yourself with wise counsel. Know that what God has placed inside you is worthy of sharing and can change the world, one person, ripple, wave, photo, podcast, essay, or idea at a time. **Overcome** the idea of failure by considering everything a lesson or an opportunity. Try things before you discount them. **Live** out your purpose by making what you know known. Someone needs what you have to offer, and they won't know you have it until you say something. Say something. **Dare** to dream and take action. Embrace the courage to pursue your passions, knowing that each step forward brings you closer to your authentic power. **BE BOLD** is my framework for continuously cultivating my creative voice and coaching my clients to do the same. You can use it, too. Whether through your strategic solutions, artistic vision, or a unique approach to solving problems in your industry, your voice is significant and meant to be heard.

Embrace your voice, cultivate it, and let it change the world.

TC Cooper *is an executive coach, attorney, and trusted friend who empowers leaders to cultivate their creative voices. With over two decades of experience, TC helps clients transform their lives and the world through creative vision, strategic solutions, and mindful leadership.*

CoachTC.com

Valentine's Day Isn't Just for Lovers: Seven Ways to Show LOVE to Your Business

Angel Cottrell

For many around the world, February is focused on love. Traditionally, the focus is on Valentine's Day and how couples express or prove their love for one another. Regardless of your relationship status, love is a crucial ingredient for any person, situation, or venture you invest energy into and have passion for. Entrepreneurial endeavors are no different. There is a recurring piece of advice given to anyone considering opening or running a business: "You must LOVE it because the passion will have to carry you and sustain you through the inevitable struggle." This mirrors the truth about love in personal relationships. In a passionate love relationship, we must be willing to endure the ups and downs, the unknowns, the lack of clarity, the risk of heartache, and even potentially devastating loss. As Queen Elizabeth II stated, "Grief is the price we pay for love." Romantic relationships require an all-in commitment for a shot at success; the same goes for business ventures.

Businesses and organizations are material manifestations of a profound desire born in the heart. Heartfelt creative endeavors drive innovation and increase value in our lives. What you create and offer the world matters. It is an expression of your value and heartfelt love; it aligns with your purpose. February is the perfect time to check in with your heartfelt creative endeavor and evaluate if you are showing your business the love it needs. Here are seven ways to do that:

1. **See the best in your business.** Focus on the positive aspects and strengths of your business as we do with those we love. Recognize its achievements, no matter how small, and use them as motivation to push forward. Celebrate milestones and victories to maintain a positive outlook. Commit to continuous improvement by

acknowledging and addressing areas that need to be changed or enhanced. Establish a plan to increase positive outcomes to ensure forward progression.

2. **Opportunity vs. obligation.** Approach your business with a mindset of opportunity rather than obligation. Embrace the opportunities for growth, innovation, and success rather than treat them as burdensome duties. This shift in perspective can reignite your passion and drive. An effective way to accomplish this mindset adjustment is to change your language from "have to" to "get to." When we state, "I have to . . . " we may feel as if external forces are dictating our time and actions, and we tend to resist this infringement on our choices. When we state, "I get to . . . " we feel more in control and in charge of our time and the actions we choose to accomplish a particular task or goal. We tend to apply a more positive attitude to our actions when we feel more in control of our choices.

3. **Be committed to communication.** Open, honest, consistent communication is vital for success in every relationship and organization. Most of us believe we communicate clearly to and with others; it's the receiver of the communication that is unclear. Check in with others often and ensure the message you conveyed was received clearly and correctly. Stop assuming others interpreted your communication with the meaning you intended. Ensuring others understand the message clearly will prevent breakdowns in communication and the relationship. Whether it's with your team, customers, or partners, clear communication builds trust and strengthens relationships. Make sure to listen actively and respond thoughtfully. Invest the time to communicate consistently and honestly; the investment will pay off in dividends of trust.

4. **Stay loyal to your vision and dreams.** Stay true to the original vision and dream that inspired you to start your business. Remind yourself of your goals and aspirations regularly; let them guide your decisions and actions. Loyalty to your vision will keep you focused and motivated. Remember, the purpose of your life is to create, experience, and be the greatest version of your grandest vision. Anything and everything you put your time, effort, and energy into must align with your purpose. Reflect and evaluate if your business is creating, experiencing, and being the greatest version of its grandest vision, and if it is not, it's time to adjust and realign to the grand vision.

5. **Tell the truth—honesty is the best policy.** Transparency is key in all aspects of your business and relationships. As Simon Sinek explains, "Transparency doesn't mean sharing every detail. Transparency means sharing the context of our decisions." It is important to

identify what is working and what is not and acknowledge the wins and the challenges. Be truthful with yourself about how you feel regarding these aspects, and then share those feelings with others. Honesty with feelings fosters a culture of trust and integrity. Feelings drive action. Actions driven by feelings can either move you closer to your goals or hinder your progress. An honest evaluation of your feelings before acting ensures you are responding to changing conditions thoughtfully rather than reacting impulsively.

6. **Keep the passion alive—KISS (keep it simple).** Don't overcomplicate things. Strategically simplify your processes and procedures to maximize your time and maintain clarity, organization, and focus. Keeping things simple helps you avoid unnecessary stress and burnout. Being in a more relaxed state helps you stay passionate and keeps the spark alive.

7. **Trifecta: time, attention, and affection.** Dedicate consistent quality time with undivided attention and loving affection to your business and important relationships. Time is one of the most valuable commodities an entrepreneur has at their disposal. Just like a personal relationship, your business needs your undivided attention and care. Invest time nurturing it, pay attention to its changing needs, and show affection by appreciating its unique qualities and vital contributions to your success.

By showing your business love in these seven ways, you can ensure it remains a thriving and fulfilling endeavor. Your heartfelt commitment and passion will not only sustain you through challenges but will lead to greater success and fulfillment in all aspects of your endeavor and life.

Angel Cottrell, CEO of Apollo Consultancy Group, combines strategy-driven consulting with executive coaching to help entrepreneurs actualize their dreams. Angel is an educator who has taught business and leadership to over 10,000 students, a master builder of programs that advance organizational missions, and most importantly, the proud mom of Alexandra.

ApolloConsultancyGroup.com

SUCCESSFULLY DEFYING INDUSTRY AND GENDER STEREOTYPES

Karen Taylor Dade

My journey as a global hospitality executive and architect started with a life drawing class. The power of observation demanded in life drawing taught me to see intimate details and nuances of light and shade. As a naturally observant and empathetic person, my internal radar is always searching for cues to deliver better outcomes across all spectrums of opportunity.

As a fifteen-year-old waitress, I was struck by the choreography of people and spaces and observed the symbiotic relationship between concept vision, architecture, and operational success, but my aspiration to study hotel management with architecture in the 1970s was met with both skepticism and sexism. Upon graduation, I was told I could be anything I wanted to be. I was also bluntly told that hotel management and architecture weren't careers for women. Nevertheless, I graduated Dux with a diploma in hotel management, but unlike my male contemporaries, I didn't receive a single job offer. Undeterred, I applied to study architecture at RMIT, citing my William Angliss results and how a lack of operational insight impacted the long-term viability of highly invested hospitality projects. I received a letter of offer, and I sought subject advice from the head of RMIT Architecture. In my second year, I discovered I'd been deliberately misled; my core subjects in year two did not align.

As they say, everything happens for a reason. To pay for my studies, I worked at a hotel in a small regional town in Victoria, where the owner invited me to review his multi-million-dollar expansion plans to meet strong weekday occupancy. I submitted a new proposal highlighting missed opportunities to optimize his investment, purposefully targeting an emerging market for destination weddings and special occasion venues and adding a chapel and wedding suites. Knowing any change at this late stage was expensive, I forecast a conservative 100% increase in his projected budget. I was appointed to my first role as general manager of the hotel to implement the full execution of my proposal, doing everything I was told, as a woman, I could not do. I was just twenty-four.

Billy Ocean's song, "When the Going Gets Tough, the Tough Get Going" became my mantra. Driving my team's resilience whilst highlighting the importance of tapping into our innate primeval instincts, I taught them not just to see but to look, not just to hear but to listen, and then to act and own. With this expansion, I became group general manager of Australia's tenth largest hotel group and one of the first women to hold such a position. However, the global financial crisis hit in 1989, and the Australian hotel industry suffered. I decided it was time for a new adventure and accepted the role of general manager of Turtle Island in Fiji.

A remote 600-acre island on the Blue Lagoon in Fiji, Turtle Island was one of the first of its genre: a boutique resort offering thirteen bures and little else, with guests paying US$2,000 per night, often staying up to four weeks, twice a year.

Stepping off the seaplane into the crystal-clear waters of the Blue Lagoon, I was met with a long list of complaints. I reassured the guests I was there to fix them, but their resounding "Don't change a thing" gave me pause. After a month of quiet observation, I realized *I needed to change how I did everything.* Preserving the intangible Fijian cultural and spiritual essence whilst overcoming an innate patriarchal cultural resistance, I integrated professional foundations of service to train the staff, focusing on highlighting their sensory acuity with their inherent culture of authentic personalized care to deliver life-changing memories. When I left Turtle to have my first child, their guest and industry services were world-class.

I was back in Australia with my first child, running the Melbourne National Gallery's catering and events, when the gallery closed for renovations, and I was recommended to manage the Jean Michel Cousteau Resort, one of the world's first eco resorts. The owner was at a crossroads, saying, "We're a boutique luxury resort catering to honeymooners *and* families—is that the problem?" The industry view was a resounding yes! Having heard Turtle Island guests lament that small luxury resorts didn't accept families, this was a new niche opportunity to do things differently, with the management skills and insight acquired at Turtle Island to integrate the local culture and train the staff to deliver an exceptional world-class guest experience. Within the first year, Cousteau Resort attracted international recognition and was the first recipient of Best Luxury Boutique Family Resort, World. It was the first of many subsequent international awards for diving, food, spa, and accommodations.

With success came the funds for new investments. I designed multiple projects at Cousteau, including a new villa prototype that won Best Villa Fiji and was listed last year as one of the top fifty beachfront villas in the world by *Luxury Travel*.

Questioning the status quo with vital foundational knowledge and the experience to identify opportunities with my unique creative acumen to deliver, I trained local Indigenous teams to achieve professional capability with empathy and care to showcase their point of difference. It is a triple-bottom-line approach to add value to the community as world leaders in sustainable tourism, not just a commercial success for the investor but providing life-changing career opportunities for staff and lifelong memories for guests. Kindness, empathy, and sensitivity are not barriers to success; they're essential for it.

The culmination of my international award-winning and business turnaround career was being recommended to work alongside renowned architect William McDonough on the world's first truly sustainable six-star eco-destination in the Caribbean in 2015, using all my skills to get it right, from the very first steps of concept and planning. But just like a life drawing, sometimes things don't turn out as you plan!

Karen Taylor Dade *has defied all odds to overcome industry and gender bias to achieve international award-winning acclaim and transform lives. She has applied a unique combination of skills and insight to hospitality solutions to deliver triple-bottom-line outcomes one step ahead of the bell curve.*

TaylorDade.com

Sharing My Journey: Inspiring Others through Wellness

Adriana D'Agostino

In my early thirties, I had just started a new job after finishing a four-week induction at Nestlé. The next morning, I woke in the early hours, struggling with shortness of breath, each breath feeling difficult and painful.

My husband woke up and asked if I was okay. Usually, I'd just wave it off and tell him I'd be fine, but this time, something felt different. It was 5:00 a.m., and feeling uneasy, I decided to call my husband's aunt, a retired doctor, hoping for reassurance. Instead, she advised me to head straight for emergency. I tried to stay composed, but worry began to creep in.

In the emergency room, after waiting for a while, I started feeling better and thought I could just go home. I'm typically a happy, healthy, and active person, believing I have a guardian angel always watching over me. At the time, I was at my fittest and healthiest, so I initially dismissed the incident as nothing serious and nothing to worry about, or so I thought.

When I asked if I could leave, they told me no and that I was going to be admitted for deep vein thrombosis (DVT) and pulmonary embolism (PE). On top of that, they said I was lucky to be there because people with my symptoms and multiple blood clots in the lungs often arrive DOA, which stands for "dead on arrival." I was like, wait, what? It took me a moment to process that it meant exactly what it said.

Honestly, I never thought this could happen to me. I had always felt blessed; life had always been good, and I'd never faced a serious hospitalization before. Sure, I'd had chickenpox as a kid, but otherwise, I was healthy and strong. This was a real shock! Initially, I didn't fully grasp the severity of my condition.

Even when they explained that I needed blood thinners, was warned about the risk of activities that could cause cuts or bruises—meaning no more contact sports, something I loved—and advised reducing Vitamin K-rich foods like asparagus, broccoli, and spinach, which were staples in my diet, I realize now that I was in denial.

I began adjusting to my new reality. Years later, when I experienced a second DVT, followed by escalating wrist pains that soon spread to various parts of my body, I was diagnosed with rheumatoid arthritis (RA). The pain became debilitating, disrupting my sleep, preventing me from driving, and making even simple tasks like lifting a glass extremely painful. Exhausted and in constant pain, exercise was my only respite, albeit temporary.

My doctors and specialists prescribed steroids to reduce inflammation, followed by long-term medications that had potential side effects like retinal damage.

At this pivotal moment, I decided to explore holistic approaches to enhance my health. Pursuing studies at the Institute of Integrated Nutrition (IIN), I became a certified integrative holistic health coach, transforming my health journey and my life.

The rheumatoid arthritis medication effectively relieved the pain and inflammation. However, as I integrated additional health-improving measures, I noticed their combined benefits. After discussions with my doctor, I concluded it was appropriate to stop taking the medication. It has been over ten years since my last RA flare-up, and I have stayed off medication by adopting a healthy lifestyle. This includes opting for a gluten-free, sugar-free, soy-free, and dairy-free diet, while striving to maintain balance in all aspects of my life.

More recently, approximately two years ago, I received a diagnosis of splenic marginal zone non-Hodgkin lymphoma (SMZL) following months of unexplained severe stomach pains, dizziness, sweating, and vomiting.

Initially, my GP dismissed my concerns, stating, "We can't find anything despite all tests being conducted." Fortunately, a new doctor reviewed my case and conducted additional tests, leading to a consultation with a hematologist, who identified abnormal cells in my spleen. We discussed various treatment options, including the potential removal of my spleen and chemotherapy. Curious about non-invasive alternatives, I sought advice from the medical team, and it was decided that a series of immunotherapy sessions was the best option for me. Throughout this journey, I asked numerous questions about the treatment, its implications, and the origins of my condition, even though I was told I was a unique case. I also inquired about alternative therapies and lifestyle adjustments, although their effectiveness lacked scientific validation. Thankfully, my specialists and doctors were supportive, taking the time to listen, understand my perspective, and patiently explain my diagnosis and treatment plan.

Battling autoimmune challenges while navigating early menopause and lymphoma further shaped my holistic approach to health. Through lifestyle changes, diet adjustments, exercise, meditation, and holistic practices, I found relief and vitality, and after twenty-plus years, I am thrilled to say I am also off blood thinning medication under the guidance of my naturopath.

If I can share some wisdom from my own personal holistic health journey, it would be this: being well-informed is crucial for your health and well-being. Don't shy away from asking questions, challenging the doctor's recommendations, and exploring both conventional and alternative options. Seek a second opinion when needed. Ensure your healthcare provider supports your decisions and genuinely cares about your health and happiness.

I was lucky to have received such amazing support and care, and I strongly believe everyone deserves the same. That's a big part of why I became a health coach—your health is far too precious to leave to chance!

Today, as a holistic health coach, I'm committed to empowering others to achieve vibrant health through simple lifestyle changes and balanced well-being practices.

Wishing you vibrant health wherever you find yourself in life's journey.

Adriana D'Agostino's *health journey began in her mid-thirties with a sudden medical emergency. Discovering the importance of sleep, diet, exercise, happiness, and managing stress transformed her approach to well-being. As a health coach, she is driven to share these insights, be a part of a movement, and positively impact others' lives.*

AdrianaDAgostino.com

Wisdom to Heal Emotional Pain

Crystal Derksen

Imagine a life where the weight of emotional pain is lifted, no longer holding you captive. Instead, you stand tall, feel empowered and strong, with a sense of freedom and liberation that radiates like a beacon of light in the darkness.

Millions of people are trapped in a cycle of emotional pain, feeling lost in the shadows without a clear direction or beacon to guide them. I was one of them, stuck in feelings of self-doubt and fear with no clear escape from the emotional storm that had clouded my mind and heart since childhood. I was convinced there was something wrong with me, that I was broken beyond repair, accepting the limitations I perceived.

There's a quote that rings true for me: "When the student is ready, the teacher will come," and that's exactly what happened. I knew what I was doing wasn't working, so I pressed through my fear to go beyond my comfort level. Growing up in a conservative environment, I was afraid of being labeled a heretic, a new-age thinker, or worse, that God would condemn me for doing something wrong or deviating from the traditional belief system. But my desperation for relief from pain and suffering gave me the courage to follow that gentle nudge, which gave me a sense of knowing that I was on the right path. It was then I began to explore the realm of energy and energy healing, and that's when everything changed.

As I began to clear the emotional pain that had held me back for so long, something miraculous happened: my physical body began to heal, too. The pain in my neck and shoulders started to disappear, and my digestive issues subsided. Our bodies follow our minds; the mind-body connection is incredibly powerful. When we focus on healing our emotional wounds, we also heal our physical bodies.

Emotional healing isn't just about getting rid of symptoms or managing emotions; it's about tuning to our souls' gentle guidance and allowing ourselves to awaken to who we are as Infinite Beings of Light. As we surrender to our true nature and allow our souls to guide us, we'll start to experience the peace, joy, freedom, clarity, and direction coming from being in alignment with our souls.

I didn't realize it at first, but I was duplicating the same patterns I'd grown up with. Religion teaches you to sacrifice yourself and give away your power to sources outside of you. That only leaves you feeling resentful and depleted.

Like many people, I was trapped in a cycle of unworthiness and people-pleasing, desperate to earn love and validation from others.

We convince ourselves that if we just do enough, say the right things, and put others first, we'll finally be loved and accepted, but this constant need for approval felt like "not enoughness"—a deep-seated fear that we're not worthy of love and acceptance just as we are.

Breaking free from a pattern requires awareness of it first, then addressing where it is stored in the body or in our energetic fields. These patterns operate in the background of our minds, shaping our perceptions and influencing our behaviors.

My process for healing meant I had to change the past memories that were hurting me. It meant I had to reframe painful experiences. It meant not caring what people thought of me. It meant acknowledging that I'm already loved and worthy of acceptance, regardless of what others think or do. It meant being in my power to communicate healthy boundaries. It meant learning how to prioritize my needs and desires so I could truly love others out of the overflow. It meant recognizing that true love and acceptance come from within, not from external validation.

The healing process required me to embrace the darkness to find the light within.

Our soul loves us so much that it will not come into agreement with the lies we believe. When we feel bad, it's not because we're inherently flawed or broken—it's because we're not aligned with our souls. That bad feeling is actually a wake-up call, urging us to re-examine our thoughts, emotions, and beliefs.

When we live in a state of brokenness, we try to fill the voids within us with external sources of validation. We seek attention, praise, or approval from others, thinking it will finally fill the holes within us, but true healing requires acknowledging that the void can't be filled by external means. It can only be filled by embracing our true selves and our inherent worthiness.

If you're reading this and feeling stuck or trapped in your own emotional pain, know that you are not alone. You have the power to create change and break free from the patterns and stories holding you back.

Take a moment to reflect on the patterns that perpetuate in your life. What lies do you believe about yourself? What holds you back from living your full potential? Then, make the conscious choice to create new narratives for yourself. Let go of who you're not and embrace who you are.

Recognize that you are worthy of love and acceptance just as you are, no matter what others think or say.

Healing is not just about fixing problems or transmuting pain—it's about embracing your true identity and living in alignment with your soul, waking up to a deep knowing that you are already healed and whole.

Crystal Derksen is a gifted and skilled intuitive. She combines spirituality, energy healing, and neuroscience to help individuals break free from energetic blockages and false perceptions. By transmuting these obstacles, she helps liberate and empower people to tap into their inner superpowers, achieving extraordinary results.

CrystalDerksen.com

It's Okay to Dream Again

Shelly Diehm

"Except ye be converted and become as little children, ye shall not enter into the kingdom of heaven . . . Whosoever therefore shall humble himself as this little child, the same is greatest in the kingdom of heaven." (Matthew 18:3–4)

I love to dream. I was raised by a dreamer. My dad once told me he enjoyed the way I delighted in the details of life. I am often aware of the simple things, the kind money can't buy, such as petals on a flower or the aroma of freshly mowed hay. After all, who can possibly get enough of an early sunrise, the kind that peaks over the top of a big red barn? It's the same feeling I get watching birds splash in puddles from the rain falling the night before. Truly, it's the simple things in life, the details, that make my heart happy.

Childlikeness is simplicity. To possess it requires a slightly slower pace. In the twenty-first century, that may seem impossible, but it isn't. It's as easy as slowing down long enough to notice the wonders of nature and allowing your heart to feel its pleasure. There is nothing more captivating than the innocence of a newborn baby. I recognize it in the birth of a calf or a litter of kittens asleep in the hay of my horse's stall. I've experienced it many times as I've held my children and grandchildren. You simply can't buy this stuff online or find it on a shelf at your local market. No human has yet to package and sell the phenomenon of our Creator. He is unmatched in imagination. It only makes sense that if you want to dream, you should learn to dream from the best!

As a child, I would daydream. I grew up in the era of *Little House on the Prairie* and *The Waltons*, airing for an hour each week on TV. They were my people. I lived a similar life and related to the love they shared and the experiences shaping their families. Inspired by

Laura Ingalls Wilder, I imagined becoming an author and writing stories about my family. Folding stacked sheets of paper, I created pages for my first book. It was hard work, complete with penciled sentences, colored drawings and a brightly painted title.

When I wasn't thinking about becoming an author, I was practicing becoming a teacher, enlisting my younger siblings as students. I even liked the idea of being a secretary because I'm a bit OCD and intrigued by the neatness of a desk, organizing files, and endless office supplies such as pens and paper clips. As a kid, anything under the sun was imaginable! I possessed a hidden power in my subconscious mind, unaware of my own creative ability.

Every role I played as a child was like an actress in a movie. I portrayed each role as if every part were true and realized I had embodied my dreams, and yet the day came when I found myself stuck. What stopped the flow?

Life. Life happened. As a wife and mother of four, I became lost in our fast-paced world, wearing many hats and simultaneously burying many parts of myself. I could no longer ignore the gnawing, empty feeling I experienced as each year crept slowly by. One day, the light within emerged; I had stopped dreaming!

The dreams I imagined as a child had reached their climax in adulthood. The person I desired, I had already become. What was left? I found myself in a funk, asking my husband, "Is this a midlife crisis?"

I landed at a doctor's office, attended Bible college, joined an online class, and hired a life coach. Everyone asked the same question: "What are you good at? What are your hobbies and interests? Who do you want to be?"

Seriously? I had just lived an entire life! How was it possible for someone like me to find herself speechless and unable to answer these simple questions?

I whispered a desperate prayer: "God, I need help," and decided to read a book on gratitude. At the time, I didn't feel grateful. In fact, I didn't feel much of anything. I needed to find something to shift my perspective, and gratitude was an obvious path, so I resolved to be thankful for the first thing that caught my eye. "Thank you, God, for blue skies and green grass," I said aloud. Suddenly, I became conscious of my surroundings in an entirely new light. No longer did the vast sky and rolling pastures appear as I always knew them to be. I became aware of the fact I was beholding an actual manifestation. The blue skies and rolling green grass were originally a dream—a dream God had dreamed! Humbled by the beauty of my surroundings, I wept. So beautiful, so simple, so profound, so very inspiring!

It was then I saw the limiting beliefs blocking my ability to dream. I was too busy living my life for others to give attention to the intuitive feelings I felt inside, too afraid to step outside of my comfort zone of familiar safety and trust my desires. I embraced the discomfort of each fear, sitting with it for a moment, allowing God to illuminate the truth until it no longer controlled me. The more I let go, the freer I became to discover parts of myself I never knew. It's been a journey I've had to embrace, not always sugar-coated, but the results are sweet like sugar. Today, I am present to receive, and I am amazed at who I've become.

If you find yourself bankrupt of dreams, it's never too late to start again. Like the lotus flower on the cover of this book, you may emerge from the murky waters of life to discover the beauty of being you. You are a powerful, creative being. Endless possibilities await you if you will only become like a little child and dream again.

Shelly Diehm *is a mother, grandmother, entrepreneur, inspirational speaker, and teacher. Born and raised in the Heartland, she founded Barnstormers and is passionate about the people of rural America. Her life mission is to make a difference, motivating others to overcome obstacles and dream again.*

ShellyDiehm.com

THAT KID

Jan Dunk

Dedicated to my boys and my kids.

I am the mother of "that kid," the one who is disruptive on a typical day and talked about at everyone's dinner table when things go awry. I knew it; I didn't need to see the other parents whispering at pick-up time or the other kids eye-rolling when my son asked a question.

As I heard the whispers and saw the disdain for the sons I love, I wanted to cry—not for me, but for my boys. I was gifted two gorgeous sons. They are beautiful, caring, compassionate, capable of so much, and intelligent beyond belief. I saw that in them every day.

Maybe not every second of every day. Let's be honest: parenting is the hardest job on the planet. Our goal is to work ourselves out of a job by helping them learn the skills they need to be independent adults who choose their own lives. No two people are the same. No two parenting journeys are the same. Some are more chaotic than others.

I wholeheartedly believe in the idiom, "Before you judge someone, walk a mile in their shoes." I don't think we should judge anyone, but for the purpose of the story, we'll ignore that word.

Those looking on with condemnation don't know what it took to get my family out the door that morning. They didn't see that my son was so anxious he vomited or that his clothing was so irritating he couldn't focus on eating breakfast. No one saw that his glass of water had been knocked over a dozen times, necessitating several outfit changes.

They don't know that if he doesn't have the right items in his bag in the proper order, he can't move forward, how many times he checked and rechecked his backpack, or the meltdown over the need for shoes. They don't know that for me, this was an easy morning, where everything went as expected, was planned for, and given ample time. On a challenging day, there were meltdowns that drained him and me of every ounce of energy his fitful and night-terror-filled sleep had allotted us, and we hadn't even made it to the car yet.

I trepidatiously dropped them at their classroom, where not only were they dealing with often tormenting compatriots, but adults who didn't understand that the clock was ticking so loudly they couldn't hear the instructions, the smell of the visiting turtle was overwhelming to the point of causing nausea, and the lights flickered in a distracting rhythm.

In the chaos of noise, light, movement, touch, and unexpected schedule changes, this boy was expected to learn new skills. He could barely distinguish the teacher's voice from the din of the classroom, let alone process, internalize, and produce proof of the day's lesson. The letters on the page would move, so he couldn't tell which word they belonged to, and the kid walking by would grab my son's paper to evoke a response just for fun. The bedlam of the lunchroom sent adults running, yet he was expected to eat. He won't. The grapes look different in the Ziplock bag than they do at home, so they might not be safe to eat.

No one saw me take him to occupational therapy to learn to write, balance, determine right from left, and gain better control over mind and body. They didn't see the hours of waiting in hospital emergency rooms because his proprioceptive sense is non-existent, and he falls, trips, and has accidents at a higher rate than other children, suffering broken bones and four concussions before the age of eleven. They didn't see the hours of specialized reading and writing programs attended. They didn't hold my son while he cried because he didn't have the gross motor skills required to play recess games. They weren't told their child would never write, read beyond grade six, ride a bike, swim, or be an independent adult. They did not walk a mile before they judged.

If they had, they would have compassion for the fight that every day brought, that my sons were tough as nails as they had overcome more by high school than most adults.

I am tremendously proud of my sons. They are now amazing young men. Do they still have frustrations? Yes, I'm sure they do, but I know that they have the resilience, skills, and determination to accomplish anything.

As a teacher, I saw many well-meaning educators struggle to support children like mine. They focused on curriculum completion over celebrating individual successes. This wasn't due to a lack of effort but a lack of understanding and tools.

As my career progressed, I leaned into teaching exceptional children, those who weren't thriving in typical classrooms. I took my Montessori training, my parenting experience, and my years of observation and developed a classroom that allows all types of learners to thrive.

Parents came to me year after year, explaining their kids were pigeonholed, left out, ostracised by faculty, bullied by peers, or told they were lazy. I called these parents the "walking wounded" because they had been battling for their child, and they, too, were exhausted and unsure of what to do next.

Students showed up to my classroom with actual trauma, kids who couldn't use a workbook without a panic attack, whose eyes welled with tears when they thought about holding a pencil, kids who had been told repeatedly they were not good enough and would never succeed.

With love, understanding, time, space, and an environment prepared for learning, these children flourish. When supported, they can learn, participate, and achieve. They are incredibly capable and intelligent and have so much to offer the world.

To thrive and be their best selves, they may need extra time, space, and compassion. I was incredibly privileged to be part of their learning journey.

In my office, a small sign read, "Be the teacher you needed" because I, too, was "that kid."

Jan Dunk *is a Montessori-trained educator with nearly two decades in independent schools, specializing in exceptional learners. Drawing from experience as a parent and teacher, Jan collaborates with educators, schools, and parents to optimize learning environments and curricula. She focuses on understanding and supporting each child's unique educational journey.*

JD@Creonova.com

THE WISDOM TO KNOW YOURSELF

Tracey Ehman

In the quiet corners of our lives, we often uncover the most profound truths. They may be hidden in the shadows or hiding in plain sight, but they are there.

Growing up as the unassuming observer, the quiet girl in the back of the class, I learned to watch the world unfold from behind my thick glasses. This vantage point, though it sometimes made me feel overlooked, became the bedrock of my journey toward self-discovery and empowerment. You can read more about this in my chapter in *Voices of the 21st Century: Women Empowered Through Passion and Purpose*, called "Being Unapologetically Me."

The epiphany that being true to myself was not a weakness but my greatest strength marked the dawn of a transformative era. Embracing the thrill of learning new skills, exploring hobbies, or venturing into new career paths became a cornerstone of my evolution. It was more than just acquiring knowledge; it was about deepening my understanding of who I am while fostering a mindset of growth and curiosity. This continuance of lifelong learning showed me that every venture beyond my comfort zone was a step closer to discovering my unique voice and carving my niche in the world.

> *"My mission in life is not merely to survive, but to thrive; and to do so with some passion, some compassion, some humor, and some style."*
> —*Maya Angelou*

As I worked my way through the non-stop challenges and opportunities life presented, the idea of legacy began to evolve. It wasn't only about what I'd leave behind; it was about the impact I could create in the here and now. Being an author in six *Voices of the 21st Century* collaborative books over the last six years has been life-changing. As an author, I was given a way to share my knowledge and my obstacles, as well as my triumphs, and shine a light on the fact that I was always changing, adjusting, and overcoming. Grasping the true essence of legacy guided me to concentrate on how I could make a meaningful difference in my community and with my loved ones. Through the lens of self-knowledge, I realized that making a difference begins with staying true to oneself and embracing one's distinct journey. The honor of putting my words on the page inspired me to create a safe place for other cancer survivors and thrivers to share their stories and leave a legacy from both the lens of a survivor and the experiences of a loved one. These stories can be found in *The Silver Lining of Cancer: 13 Courageous Women Share Their Inspirational Stories After a Life-Changing Diagnosis.*

Life's hurdles are a given, yet approaching them with resilience and grace is a conscious decision. My path taught me the wisdom to face tough times with fortitude and self-awareness. When I received the diagnosis that I had breast cancer at the young age of forty-two, my world felt as if it were falling apart. I instantly went where most people go and began to mourn for all the things I wouldn't be around to take part in. My life flashed before my eyes. However, recognizing my strengths and vulnerabilities laid a solid foundation of strength during this time and other obstacles that have come my way during my time on this Earth. It's by surmounting these challenges that I've been able to support and inspire others, demonstrating that authenticity and grace can transform hurdles into stepping stones for growth.

Reflecting on my path, I urge others to dedicate time to self-reflection and to cherish the continuous process of self-discovery. The journey ahead isn't about reaching a final destination but about valuing each step along the way. Self-awareness is a potent tool in leading a life filled with joy, health, and prosperity. It's about waking up each day with the realization that "I get to" make a difference, learn anew, and be unapologetically me. "I get to" live my best life, spend time with my family, take chances, and enjoy the goodness that is all around us.

> *"The quieter you become, the more you are able to hear."*
> *—Rumi*

In wrapping up, my ask is simple yet powerful! Let's collectively embark on this journey of self-discovery, celebrate our uniqueness, draw lessons from our experiences, and forge a legacy of positivity and growth. Remember, the road to finding your voice and making an impact isn't walked alone. Together, we can inspire, uplift, and empower one another to live our fullest lives, facing every challenge with grace and seizing every opportunity with zeal.

At the end of the day, it's about the wisdom to know ourselves, showcasing our unique, personal flair, and aiding others in doing the same. When we continue to embrace learning, evolving, and making our marks on the world, we can inspire everyone, especially the younger generation. Let's show them that almost everything they need lies within themselves, that they possess the power to take control and live their best lives. Encourage them to focus not on the "what ifs" but on the "what if nots" and how embracing chances can unlock joy and achievements beyond their wildest dreams. It is important to share the message that overcoming challenges, like a diagnosis or personal trials, can lead to a profound appreciation for life's silver linings and the strength found in gratitude.

Together, let's learn, grow, and leave a mark on the world, one day at a time.

> *"The biggest adventure you can take is to live the life of your dreams. It requires you to trust that the dots will somehow connect in your future. You have to trust in something—your gut, destiny, life, karma, whatever. This approach has never let me down, and it has made all the difference in my life."*
> —Oprah Winfrey

Tracey Ehman *is an organic marketing strategist who helps female entrepreneurs get their messages out into the world and be found online to increase their reach and income. She is also a bestselling author and podcast host.*

PartneringInSuccess.com

WISDOM DESPITE CIRCUMSTANCES

Dr. Pamela Gunter

"No matter what, never give up and don't give in. There is a purpose and a plan. Regardless of what comes your way, maintain your stance, trust the process. Just pray. The Master has the greater plan, your life is in His hand."

As a child, I had no idea these words would be the thread woven throughout my life, resonating within my spirit, soul, and body as a guiding principle, pushing me forward one day at a time, not allowing me to wallow in pity or become self-absorbed with my problems.

When I was a child, my mother passed away suddenly, leaving my father to raise four children, ages two, six, eight, and nine. I was devastated! My father never remarried but raised us up "in the discipline and instruction of the Lord" with godly principles, and he kept us in church at all times, planting the seed of a biblical foundation in our lives. I remember we did not have much. I had two pairs of shoes, one for school and one for church. They were never interchanged. As a child, I did not know what was going on. There were things I did not understand and questions that plagued me for a long time. Why had my mother passed away so young? Who had caused this to happen? How would I make it through life without my mother? What would I do? What was the purpose, and why were we in church all the time?

No matter what, never give up!

I recall feeling lost without hope. Although my father and my siblings were there along with other family members, an emptiness pervaded within me, and for years, worthlessness overshadowed me.

No matter what comes your way, just pray!

Throughout my earlier years and the tough times, I completed elementary, middle, and high school. The day of my high school graduation was melancholic. It should have been a time of great pleasure and jubilation; however, I recall sitting and twiddling my thumbs with a concern for what I was going to do next since this chapter of my life was over, and I was now moving into adulthood. Needless to say, I felt like a fish out of water, not knowing what to do or how to survive. While the other graduates were throwing their caps in the air, full of laughter, rejoicing, and celebration, there I sat with a blank stare, unprepared for the next season of life, with a lot of questions. Where would I turn? Which way should I go? How could I get to where I was supposed to be in life? What was I to do? What was the purpose, and who had the answers to my questions? There I sat in a daze, unhappy, miserable, and unsure of my future.

The Master has a greater plan. My life is in His hand.

Sometime later, God reminded me of the teaching and learning I'd received while growing up in church and going to Sunday School, Vacation Bible School, Junior Church, and Sunday Services, reading the Bible through every year, and lest I forget Momma Wallace, the spiritual woman in my life, who didn't just appear in my life by chance; there was a purpose. It was a part of the Master's plan, a divine connection. Momma Wallace was one of my mother's closest friends, and for that reason, she knew me well. She not only kept me grounded and focused in the Word of God; oftentimes, it was her persistent nudge to me through her gentle words: "You can do this. You already have in you just what you need." Purposefully, she encouraged me throughout my young adult years.

One day, I had a revelation! The Holy Spirit lived inside of me, leading, guiding, and directing me into all truth. I accepted Christ into my life as a child. It was then that I began a relationship with God that has lasted for years and matured me into the woman I am. Having a strong foundation in the Father, the Son, and the Holy Spirit was all I needed to get through the tough times and to sustain and keep me. My father gave me the groundwork by instilling in me the importance of the Church at a young age, having a relationship with God, and maintaining a solid foundation in the Word of God. Now, the rest was left up to me.

I had a choice. I could have rebelled and gone against God or continued to stay with Him, with what I knew worked through my experiences, knowledge, and judgment.

I began reading and meditating in the Word daily, not to boast that I had read the Bible through, but intentionally, with a desire to know more, to add to my understanding, to be transformed, and to bring life and light into someone else's life. My daily prayer was for wisdom and understanding because I knew that in order to get wisdom, I had to ask God. He honored my prayer. I grew in grace in the knowledge of Him and was able to apply His wisdom and word in every situation. The emptiness and worthlessness I'd experienced as a child were gone. I embraced God's Word that said, "I am fearfully and wonderfully made in His image."

Now, as I reexamine my questions from the past and get answers, I know that God is in control of everything. Although I may not understand, my job is to trust God. I've made it through the difficult times with Him because He was there then, as He is with me now. God has a purpose and a plan. Whatever the devil intends for evil, God will turn things around for His glory.

Church was where I was supposed to be to get what I needed for life.

All of my questions may not be answered until I see Jesus and behold the beauty of the Lord face to face.

Dr. Pamela Gunter *obtained a Doctor of Worship from the Robert Webber Institute of Worship Studies. She's a minister, intercessor, speaker, and founder of Power, Dominion, and Glory Ministries, who elevates, empowers, encourages, and equips others to understand their value and worth by knowing who they are and were created to be.*

PDGMinistries.com

Forget Prince Charming

Helen Hicks

I was nineteen years old when I gave birth to my first son. Despite him being born on his due date, he was a month premature with underdeveloped lungs. My water broke the night before, but the coloring of the liquid was off. It was greenish. My sister-in-law took me to the ER, and I was admitted. I was told that my baby probably had a bowel movement in utero, which was common, and there was nothing to worry about. They monitored me all night long before deciding to induce labor the next morning. The first dose of Pitocin started labor, but I didn't dilate much. The dosage was steadily increased until the pain was unbearable. Around 6 cm dilation, I requested an epidural. Relief from the pain was heavenly, but I couldn't feel my legs. By the time I reached 10 cm and the nurse prepared the bed for delivery, my legs slid into the empty space, and the rest of me began to slide down as well. I had no muscle control at all. The command to "push" was met with all the effort I could muster to control something below my waist, but it wasn't enough. The doctor requested a vacuum. He performed an episiotomy. Nurses pushed on my stomach.

My son was purple when he was born because he hadn't received enough oxygen during the delivery. The doctor and nurses leaped into immediate action, compressing, squeezing, and injecting. A few hours later, I was finally allowed to see him for the first time. As he lay in the transparent plastic hospital bassinet, he began to spit up blood. I called for the nurse, who whisked him away again. The next time I saw him, he was covered in tubes and wires. It was difficult to determine what was baby and what was machine. Without having held him even once, he was helicoptered to the NICU at Children's Hospital.

For the next week, I either borrowed my mom's car or took the city bus to visit him in the NICU. I sang him lullabies and quoted nursery rhymes for as long as I was allowed to stay. At the end of the first week, he had made tremendous progress and was being moved to a normal pediatric unit. A few days later, a nurse pulled me into a conference room to discuss his treatment plan. She said the staff was impressed by my dedication to showing up daily for the maximum allotted time and believed my son would progress even more if I took him home. He would still need IV medications twice daily for the next fourteen days, which a visiting nurse could do. The only stipulation was for me to complete an infant CPR course. Within forty-eight hours, my son was home for the first time. And for the first time, I was a full-time single mom.

I could only imagine what it was like for him to be so little, not understanding what had happened to him or why his arm was strapped to a board. The discomfort and pain he experienced. He cried often and only seemed to be consoled when held. The first time I tried to take a shower with him at home left us both on the floor, soaked in tears. I rocked him to sleep, placed him in the bassinet located outside the shower, and turned the water on. He screamed to the point that it scared me. I put the automatic rocker in the bathroom. He screamed. I tried both previous methods with the shower already on, so the noise didn't scare him. He screamed. I tried singing to him while I showered. He screamed. After numerous failed attempts, I sat on the bathroom floor crying and telling myself how much easier this would be if anyone at all was there to help me. I thought how unfair it was that I was the only parent there to bear the burden. Where was Prince Charming and his white horse when I needed him? Then it hit me: no one was coming. Not that day or any day. My only choice was to decide if I was going to let both of us die because it was too hard or figure it out. And in the grand scheme of it all, this part, taking a shower, was easy. If I couldn't figure this out, then why had I chosen to be a mother at all? I sat on the floor a few moments more. I allowed myself to have one last cry and pity party before it was time to be a big girl, a single mom. I told myself that once I got off that floor, it was time to figure things out.

Wishing for something different wasn't going to solve anything. I had to figure out how to do it. And I did. It took a few tries, but I eventually learned to put my son's baby carrier on the bathroom floor, line it with two towels and an open diaper, wrap his arm in a plastic bag and receiving blanket, put both of us in the shower, wash him first then let the warm water relax him to sleep, place him in the carrier with the diaper loosely taped, fold over the towels, put an extra folded towel on top, then wash myself in peace.

I was nineteen when I decided my circumstance did not determine my ability to thrive. This was one of countless wins and a single circumstance in a sea of many. I haven't felt like I've won every time, but I have survived. Each success has given me something I needed for the next part of my journey. I hope these words encourage you in your journey. Being a single mom is not a badge of disgrace but a symbol of resilience and ingenuity. Be your own hero. Forget Prince Charming!

***Helen Hicks** is a dedicated mental health professional who has spent nearly three decades making a positive impact in the field. With a deep passion for helping individuals and families navigate the complexities of mental health and parenting, she has established herself as a trusted authority in her areas of expertise.*

HelenVHicksCounseling.com

SHINE ON

Zan Johns

"Dwell on the beauty of life. Watch the stars, and see yourself running with them."
—Marcus Aurelius

The Women Speakers Association's (WSA) Women Poets SHINE community launched in June 2024. This community of light is a safe gathering place for women poets and the culmination of WSA Founder Gail Watson's and my intentional waltz. Its formation is similar to a lotus flower's blossoming journey. There are many exceptional poetry societies and platforms offering a plethora of services. What sets SHINE apart is its affiliation with WSA and its women-only membership.

Star metaphors are commonly used to describe life events and people. A physical star is a gaseous celestial body that draws light from its own internal sources. People who yield to their inner source of light are called stars or luminaries. They are uniquely gifted and tend to stand out in a crowd. A star will always shine as light cannot be disputed or denied. Especially in darkness, absolute or symbolic, stars cannot be concealed.

I am a luminary who yields to my talents and naturally gravitates toward other luminaries. One of my most remarkable revelations is that the engagement is not about me. Instead, it is about aligning with those who share my mission in the interest of the greater good. We are deeply anchored in the foundations of our purpose. We move in pairs or clusters, just like stars, too driven and selfless to be contained. Our attraction is derived from our commonality and placement on the same inspirational frequency. When our sparks unite, and our expressions burst in truth, together, we shine more brightly.

In my former workplace of twenty-nine years, I was sometimes called a servant leader. I have been referred to as a North Star in recent years. Although I was humbled by these remarks, it was not until recently that I began to embrace and seize that merit. It wasn't as clear before; however, I was aware that I embodied an inner glow. Others tended to perceive my ability and light long before I could say it loudly. I'm following the steps that were divinely commanded for my life long ago. I strive to help others and not to gratify myself.

I started writing poetry in 1976. At the time, I was unaware of my transformation to come. I followed the path convergent to roads traveled by poets like Nikki Giovanni, Maya Angelou, Mary Oliver, Langston Hughes, and Robert Frost. On a symbolic creative pilgrimage, my writing flourished along with a profound awareness of my faith and beliefs. I have lived meaningful experiences that I muse about in written expressions of my soul. My poems meet readers where they are, allowing them to reflect on their own spirit and beliefs. Since 2020, I have produced three poetry collections and a journal, coauthored four collaborative books, and co-edited three poetry anthologies.

I am forever changed. A quote from *Worlds Collide* says, "When two worlds collide, you can't remain unchanged." In Spring 2023, Gail Watson inquired about how WSA might assist with my literary efforts, an example of how WSA members are supported and valued. While her intention was to share and assist with my dreams, what I analyzed was how we could assist each other. I seek success-win partnerships that are equally gratifying.

Upon thoughtful reflection, I recognized that I was uniquely positioned to share my experience of thriving in two distinct worlds: poetry and WSA. My success as a poet is as fulfilling as my success as a four-time contributing author in the *Voices of the 21st Century* books. Realizing that my destiny is both, I felt deeply enlightened. Worlds colliding in modern slang is viewed as a conflict or clash; I viewed the opportunity to collaborate with WSA's world of women's empowerment as ideal.

My proposal featured strategies for promoting poetry within WSA. My goal was to explore opportunities to attract and engage emerging and esteemed women poets to the organization. When you plant a seed with Gail, you can anticipate the emergence of a mighty oak tree. She responded with this elaborate vision of a community that encourages women poets to shine:

Haven for the creative souls who use the power of words to uplift, empower, and inspire, our community is an inclusive space where women poets from diverse backgrounds and experiences can connect, collaborate, and support each other in their poetic journeys.

At its core, the Women Poets Community aims to cultivate a vibrant network of women who share an ardor for poetry. Whether you're a seasoned poet or just starting out, this community is here to nurture your poetic spirit and provide a platform to enhance your skills and amplify your voice.

My collaboration with WSA began after a year of enthusiastic discussions that led to my appointment as poet laureate and the creation of SHINE. In this role, I compose the dedication poems for *Voices of the 21st Century*, which involves my active participation during the publication process. I incorporate the collective insight gained from my coauthors and their respective stories into the poem. Vincent van Gogh said, "One can speak poetry just by arranging colors well." I counter with, "One can paint a masterpiece just by the thoughtful placement of select words." I paint masterpieces for *Voices of the 21st Century*. Women Poets SHINE is an inspirational masterpiece. In this community, our ultimate objective is to present notable women poets to the world. With WSA's supportive team of women who make things happen, we are well on our way.

Zan Johns *is the world-class author of* Poetic Forecast, After the Rainbow, Encore, Voices of the 21st Century *(2021–2024) and* What Matters Journal. *She's also co-editor of three poetry anthologies and an editor of* Fine Lines. *Her expressions appear in numerous publications. Zan is the poet laureate for Women Speakers Association.*

ZanExpressions.com

His Hands and Feet

Lauren Kirby

I didn't know. There's no way I could know. Looking back now, boy, do I know! A childhood trauma led to a slow, methodical introduction to a life of volunteerism, serving the greater good. My transformation began in West Africa as a four-year-old, wearing my favorite Mary Jane, black patent leather shoes, and racing with my brother, which resulted in my crashing through a sliding glass door. As my right arm instinctively rose to shield my face, the shattered glass slashed the artery in the crook of my elbow and wrist of my right arm. Surgical intervention was hours away in Stuttgart, Germany. I should have died that day, but I didn't.

I grew up in an atheistic family as the different one, not like the others. I now know the difference was because I was set apart and called in 1990 to be a child of God when I asked Jesus into my life. My heart and life were His all along. I just didn't know it yet.

As a new Christian, I prayed for my gifts and talents to be revealed and to know where He wanted me to serve. "Where there is great suffering" landed hard in my spirit. Looking back, my traumatic injury, life experiences, and volunteerism were my training fields. He led me to these experiences, each building on the other with an increasing level of complexity and severity.

My simple prayer signaled that the years of grooming and training had prepared me to say, "YES, I will go" wherever He needed me. The Bible cites many references of God communicating through dreams, and He still does! After my prayer, I received five vivid dreams over nine years, which provided a preview and a hint as to where He wanted me. I was being asked to do something that I didn't want to do, something that scared me and not just anyone can do. Secretly hoping He would change His mind, I asked again if He was sure that was where I was supposed to serve. He let me know that, yes, that was where He wanted me and that I should trust Him. I don't know if He rolled His eyes, but it certainly would have been justified!

We all have gifts and talents that can serve those in need. We can show kindness, generosity, empathy, and care for people who have real, scary, painful, and permanent challenges, or just be available to sit, hold a hand, and listen.

My injury and recovery set in motion deep compassion for those struggling with life's challenges. My volunteerism included: from ages eight to thirteen, cared for a paralyzed neighbor; at fourteen, volunteered with profoundly handicapped children; from eighteen to the present, began serving in the volunteer fire service at local and state levels; and from thirty-three to the present, became a hospice volunteer, trainer, speaker, and advocate. Later, I served as a board member of a homeless service non-profit for three years and a philanthropist, supporting a local alternative high school for ten years.

Here's what my volunteer journey has taught me:
- You are special and made for more than just being a consumer of what the world offers. Your gifts are needed because there are people who have real and immediate needs, and Jesus isn't physically here anymore to walk to their bedsides, hold their hands, and wipe their brows. When there is a need or a softly spoken prayer, He looks across the kingdom to see who is willing to go and be His hands and feet. He looks for people who have a heart that is open and caring but who may not yet know yet that this is His heart. His hand is on you before you feel its touch, but trust me, you will feel it when the time comes.
- You can help de-mystify the scary times in life with what you know and learn. By slowing down, prioritizing, and focusing on the need, you'll find that you do have a few hours each week to volunteer. During these times, you'll realize you're prepared, have the answers, and want to help. You can hold a hand, give a comforting hug as soft cries land on your shoulder, help the homeless find work, read to children, or do dishes for the elderly. There's nothing more humbling than meeting someone who has questions (and you have the answers) or someone who is alone (and you can help fill their time).
- When you make a difference for someone, you will be called an angel, family, and a friend. You will become a better person

because you've carved out a small piece of your life and heart for a stranger who will never forget you and how you made them feel better and stronger.
- Yes, God has His hand on you, even if you don't know it yet. He's bringing people and experiences across your path so you're ready to fulfill the service He designed just for you. The cause that breaks your heart is your signal to engage. I'm glad it was revealed to me while I was able to deliver on it. I can't imagine being on my death bed, realizing God had called me but I'd missed the signs.

For over thirty years, I've been honored to de-mystify the end-of-life process for my family and patients in homes, hospitals, assisted living, and memory care units. Through hands-on care, public speaking, training, one-on-one listening, and family coaching, His hands and feet were given motion. It's been one of the most profound joys of my life to see how my journey, prayers, and service have come to pass exactly as He planned and why He saved me at four years old. Feelings from my childhood about being different have long since dissolved; I was designed to be different. When the phone rings, and a shaky voice says, "Can you help me?" they get my time and attention. Needs are everywhere if you just look closely.

Lauren Kirby *lives in Northern Virginia. She's the author of* Preview to Destiny, *works as a risk and audit manager, and believes everyone has God-given talents they can share to make the world a better place, one need at a time.*

PreviewToDestiny.com

Speak Inclusive Words to Hear Inclusive Words

Paula M. Kramer

In *Women Empowered Through Passion and Purpose,* Gail Watson wrote about "a powerful ripple effect across the globe." Wise women understand that our word ripples come back to us.

My mother tried to kill me twice because I was her second daughter instead of her first son. The words she'd always heard were that she needed a son to prove herself a worthy woman. My sisters followed our mother's example. Their negativity has rippled back to them in my various writings and podcast interviews.

The staff at my all-girl high school spoke mostly judgmental and punitive words. Alumnae hear positive words only if we donate money. Our accomplishments mean nothing if we don't prove our loyalty through donations. The staff's negative words created negative ripples for both the school and for me. Only 3% of alumnae donate money to the school because 97% of us refuse to support its negative word ripple. One of my classmates had a smile that helped me survive the terrors of my childhood. Decades later, I told that classmate what her smile still meant to me. Our high school's negative words had turned her comforting and terror-suspending smile into a judgmental and punitive frown.

While in college, I watched a female television talk show host betray a female guest on-air, speaking words that made the guest responsible for male thoughts and actions: if the guest was raped, it would be her fault. I wrote my master's thesis about female talk show hosts after watching five talk shows a day for two years. Each host repeated four cultural themes of betrayal between women: Women as Mothers, Women and Their Appearance, Women as Deviants, and Teenage Girls as Threats to Society. I realized I had spoken judgmental words about other girls and women along with the talk show hosts.

I changed my word ripples with four girl mindsets. **Girl Grit:** the courage to create equality for all girls and women, including girls and women who create inequality for you. **Girl Goodwill:** the determination to approach all encounters involving other girls and women with sincere approval and support for their positive words and actions. **Girl Gumption:** the wisdom to admit that men deny equality to women who see men as inferior. **Girl Gems:** positive words supporting other girls and women by putting a shine on their skills and accomplishments.

If you listen, you will hear wise women speaking positive words.

Nina Elaine Borum, Women as Mothers: Nina is a single mom, an adoptive mom and a foster mom. On *The Resilient Mother* podcast with host Tiffany Lorraine Galloway, she speaks positive words to mothers who surrender their children to foster care. She recognizes that too many mothers don't have the support they need to keep their children safe. She says, "I want you to know you don't love your child any less if you made a choice that put them in a safer situation."

Dolly Parton Fans, Women and Their Appearance: In November 2023, Dolly Parton wore a modified version of a Dallas Cowboys cheerleader outfit while performing during the half-time show for a game between the Cowboys and the Washington Commanders. Critics wrote judgmental words on social media. Positive words celebrated Parton for enjoying herself instead of acting old.

Grade School Classmate Debra, Women as Deviants: In grade school, several girls brutally teased another girl about her unusual name. I did not participate in the teasing, but I said nothing to stop the teasing. Classmate Debra did. She asked the teasers how they would feel if someone teased them relentlessly about their names. The teasing stopped, and I witnessed a girl taking positive control in the small space of one situation.

Chelsey Goodan, Teenage Girls as Threats to Society: Goodan wrote the book *Underestimated: The Wisdom and Power of Teenage Girls*. Teenage girls live with more restrictions and expectations than any other segment of society. Learning how to value teenage girls could ripple into adults learning how to value themselves.

My favorite word ripple example comes from a kindergartner. I picked my first-grade granddaughter up from school once a week. One cloudy day, I arrived early and waited outside the school doors. The kindergartners came out first and walked into the parking lot. One little girl had an umbrella she showed to her friends. When light rain began to fall, the school adults told the kids to move underneath the portico where I was waiting. Umbrella Girl stood near me and opened her umbrella.

The girl closest to Umbrella Girl joined her underneath the umbrella. Three other girls crowded in. A boy standing nearby squeezed himself into the crowd, saying he wanted to join, too. One of the girls shouted, "Get out!" Umbrella Girl announced, "I want him to stay!" The umbrella crowd dispersed moments later. Tongue-tied me tried to put together words to tell this very young equality advocate how proud I was of her. Amazing me yet again, Umbrella Girl looked up at me and said, "It's *my* umbrella!" I agreed with her: "It's *your* umbrella."

A kindergartner had taken positive control in the small space underneath her umbrella and started an inclusive word ripple bringing light to the world. She taught inclusion to the girls and invited inclusion from the boy. Umbrella Girl had put "I want him to stay!" into Included Boy's ears. With those words in his mind, Included Boy now has a reason to say, "I want her to stay!" whenever he takes positive control in his small spaces.

If a kindergartener can take positive control in her small space and ripple inclusion with one short sentence, so can adult you. The words you speak about other females can go into male ears and come out of their mouths about you.

What small spaces do *you* control?

What short sentences could you speak to teach inclusion and invite inclusion?

Start a ripple of inclusion for yourself by putting words of inclusion into male ears, contributing to a powerful ripple effect of men including women across the globe.

Paula M. Kramer *is a soft skills mastermind who has extensively researched relationships between girls, relationships between women, and their relationships with themselves. Website pages: Girl Grit, Girl Goodwill, 4 Girl Mindsets, Speaking Equality, Leading for Change Through Choices, and SOPY Strategy for Breaking Glass Ceilings. Facebook pages: Women Speaking Equality and Girl Goodwill.*

SpeakingFromTriumph.com

Beyond Grief: Rising from Ashes

Zeenath Kuraisha

This chapter is dedicated to anyone deeply impacted by the loss of a loved one.

Success is often celebrated, but the unseen battles, immense grief, and misunderstood pain are rarely acknowledged. My life was no different. Outwardly, I appeared successful and happy, but beneath the surface, I faced numerous challenges, the most devastating being the loss of my son.

It was at a time when I was consumed with building my new business amidst so many financial struggles and personal challenges. One seemingly ordinary night, I tucked my son into bed, unaware it would be the last time. By morning, my world was shattered: my son was gone, leaving a void no words could fill.

Life changed irrevocably. My journey through darkness began. The burden of grief was overwhelming, as if a piece of my soul had been torn away. My path to healing and acceptance was just starting, shaped by immense pain and loss.

My grieving family turned their blame towards me. As a woman, I was expected to be solely responsible for anything that happened in the house.

A sense of guilt overwhelmed me as if I were responsible for this loss—if only I had been there to fight the god of death that night. I questioned my parenting, wondering if I had failed as a mother. A thousand "what ifs" tormented me, deepening my despair.

I attended functions seeking normalcy, but people judged me, wondering how I could be normal and have the face to attend such events and a heart to enjoy. My extended family believed I had forgotten my son and was heartlessly living my life.

As if the loss and guilt weren't enough, while still trying to get over the initial shock, my relatives started spreading rumors. They had no idea what I was enduring, and they filled the void with their own narratives.

They didn't understand the emptiness or the strength it took to hide my pain. They didn't see the countless nights I'd cried, the moments I'd spoken to my son's memory, how I'd sought solace in his absence. They couldn't grasp the weight of the guilt and grief I carried or the immense effort it took to get out of bed each morning. Instead of support, I was isolated, and all fingers pointed at me, leaving me to navigate my dark path alone.

My journey through grief was filled with unseen struggles and silent battles, but I persevered, finding strength amidst the sorrow.

One day, I felt the urge to reclaim my sanity, snap out of the sadness, and focus on the present and future I wanted. I faced two choices: continue grieving or embrace reality and move forward for my family's sake. The choice was clear.

I found comfort in my faith, believing my son was in a better place and making the most of every moment by embracing life's unpredictability. I accepted that everything happens for a reason, even if it was not immediately clear. In other words, I trusted God. Focus became my lifeline as I worked to shift from pain to acceptance. Grief lingered like a shadow, but I refused to let it overpower me and gave priority to my family's happiness. Accepting the loss was crucial, but so was considering the well-being of my loved ones, who needed me now more than ever. Life goes on, even when it feels at a standstill, and we couldn't let this tragedy drown us. I also focused on what was possible and believed in the possibility of happiness and fulfillment. Life can still be beautiful, even after a loss.

People's opinions are shaped by their fears and understanding, but their words don't define our realities. Focus on your own healing and growth. You don't need to explain yourself or seek anyone's empathy or sympathy. Only someone who has walked in our shoes can fully grasp the loss. Only you can truly help yourself. Accept that some things are beyond our control. I reminded myself that I am human and cannot be blamed for what is destined. Not all mothers can be perfect 24/7. People will always play the blame game; we must ignore it and learn to move on.

I became a pillar of strength for my family, realizing that sometimes, you must take on the world alone, and that's okay. How I saw myself and my situation was crucial. I was not a victim or a villain—I was a mother dealing with immense pain. I focused on positive moments and joyful memories of my son, adopting an attitude of resilience.

There is presence in absence. Losing someone doesn't mean they don't exist. They live on in our minds, co-existing with us. We see them in every little thing. They are always with us, MORE than before.

I also learned to respond with positivity instead of letting negativity take hold when reminded of my loss. I realized that I couldn't change the past, but I could shape my future, so I channeled my energy into my business, transforming it into an award-winning venture.

Healing is a gradual process. Embrace each day without rushing. Look ahead with hope. Set small, achievable goals that will provide purpose and direction. Engage in activities that bring happiness and connect with supportive, non-judgmental people.

Grief is a part of life and not its end. There is hope, healing, and a future waiting. We shouldn't feel guilty for living fully or being happy. Through pain and loss, we can find a way to rise again.

I'm sharing my moments to help others find strength and resilience, even when every step feels impossible.

***Zeenath Kuraisha**, founder and CEO of APACSMA, The E-University for Sales, is a visionary sales leader with over twenty-five years of global experience in inside sales, customer excellence, and sales education. Recognized as one of the Top 50 Asian Women Leaders and Executive of the Year for Education, she drives impactful, sustainable, and customer-focused sales practices.*

APACsma.com

SECRETS TO SUCCESS OVER FOUR DECADES

Marsha Lake

*Dedicated to my dad/mentor for his guidance
on my journey*

My business journey has spanned over four decades! Where did that time go?

Did I believe that in my seventies, I would be continually motivated and inspired to continue on my journey? I have to say **YES** because of my passion, determination, dedication, and honest **desire** to help businesses and individuals and make them feel special and more confident about themselves, which remains to this day.

So, how could I help you, the reader, learn more about my business journey to motivate and help you to reach your goals? What pieces of advice and inspiration could I give you? What could I share to help you?

Tip 1: Listening and Communicating. I believe that listening and communicating are the keys to becoming successful in your business. Having operated a business for four decades now, I have learned to be a sounding board for my clients, being a true professional who shows them empathy and respect. Most importantly, being visible, down-to-earth, honest, and transparent to new and existing clients.

Did I learn all of this from the beginning? No, I didn't. My Dad-and-No-1-Mentor had operated a successful printing business over many years and was always a phenomenal resource to me, especially when I commenced the business. I began attending many networking meetings with like-minded business owners, talking, working, collaborating, and gaining amazing inspiration from them.

Tip 2: Finding a Mentor. As a small business owner, it is, at times, lonely up the top, and having a business network to collaborate with is invaluable. I recommend this tip to all of you. Finding a mentor you feel comfortable with is important and very helpful, someone you can "bounce off" ideas with, especially when you are building up your business.

I have mentored many clients over the years, ascertaining the specific assistance they require and how we can help them, providing suggestions on streamlining their businesses, and discussing other services we feel will be beneficial to them. At that time, we discussed our large network of businesses in other industries we collaborated with and who we could personally recommend. Having personal recommendations is vital to all business owners. This enables clients to gain additional trust from us, knowing we are alleviating their frustrations in all areas of business.

Tip 3: Good Quality Clients. There are many ways you can find new and "good quality" or "target" clients and, more importantly, sustain a long and mutually beneficial relationship with them. Over the years, I have been very privileged to nurture and gain the trust and respect of our clients with professionalism and our expertise. Our clients have felt comfortable to send through many written and verbal testimonials. For me personally, this is a testament to being a long-time business owner and how I have strived for continued longevity and good quality ongoing working and personal relationships with our clients to remain a successful business owner.

How do you want to present yourself so that prospective clients will want to work with you? Being visible, transparent, and honest are what come to mind and developing new ways of presenting and/or reinventing yourself in a positive way to gain new business and retain your existing good quality clients.

Do you believe that to present yourself, you need to talk continually for five minutes, explaining what you do and how you can assist them? *No!* A prospective client wants to know how you can help them in a few words. They want the information you supply to them to be succinct and relevant to your areas of expertise.

When it comes to presenting yourself, can you explain this in six words? I recently reinvented my business introduction from "I have a secretarial and administration business" to "I am a visual presentation and transcription expert." This has made a remarkable difference. Business owners now immediately understand which areas of business we focus on and how we can assist them. Once you have gained this interest, the prospective client will feel more comfortable asking you further questions about their requirements, and you will then have the opportunity to expand on your services.

Another quick tip for you, and an important part of presenting yourself, is to empower your passion in the way you speak to them. Passion is infectious, and your prospective and existing clients will feel your enthusiasm and expertise shine through!

Tip 4: Operating a Business. Operating a business—has this been easy? Absolutely not. Have I succeeded in everything I wanted to achieve? Absolutely not! Every business can improve and learn. No one is perfect—and I put my hand up in that regard—far from it! But talking and gaining expertise from others you collaborate with and defining the obstacles will help you become successful.

Tips to Remember: Listen to your new and/or existing clients' needs. Communicate with your clients and business networks on a regular basis by telephone, emails, coffee get-togethers, lunches, and Zooms. Be there to lend a helping hand and professional advice at all times. Continually network and collaborate with other businesses. Always listen and learn from your business network about the challenges they face or have faced in the past to continually educate yourself.

My business journey stands as a testament to resilience, determination, and the transformative power of turning adversity into opportunity. Alleviating stress and ensuring seamless delivery to our clients has shone a light on the professional demands of operating a successful business.

I hope my tips and suggestions have been helpful to you.

Always remember: *You are not alone—there are other business owners who can help you!*

Prepare to embark on a journey. Believe in yourself, and there will be many boundless possibilities for those who dare to pursue their dreams and goals!

Marsha Lake is a visual presentation and transcription expert with four decades of experience operating a successful secretarial and administrative business. Her honest, down-to-earth, hard-working, confidential and professional approach has gained repeated testimonials, trust, and friendships from clients that she has had the privilege of working with over the years.

MLSS.com.au

Empowered Women Empowering Women

Gloria Manchester

At a young age, I believe God set me on a path to become a fearless warrior for abused girls and women.

Since my sisters were twelve and fifteen years older, I was raised as an only child. When I was five years old, we lived in a French-Canadian Catholic community with a lot of families that had many children and were quite poor. Because I had no siblings, I loved sharing everything I had with those kids, including my toys and food. My best friend, Martha, who was also five, lived across the street and came from a family of twelve. Their mother had abandoned them.

One day, I walked into her house to play and saw her father naked and on top of her. I ran home and told my mother, who called Child Protective Services. The father was arrested, the kids were all taken away, and I lost my best friend.

This event was buried in my subconscious for years but has impacted my life in so many ways. I've always been bold. As a teenager, I often stood up for girls who were being bullied. Then, as an adult, I developed my spiritual awareness and participated in personal growth seminars. This deepened my passion for making a difference with girls who have been exposed to sexual, physical, or emotional abuse.

I went on a mission! I founded a nonprofit organization and invited a group of thirteen women leaders to a retreat in Palm Springs. I told them what I'd witnessed as a five-year-old. Shockingly, we discovered that eleven of the thirteen women who were sharing their stories had either been raped or sexually or physically abused as children. This resulted in a unanimous decision: the nonprofit would focus on empowering teen girls who'd been abused to rise above their circumstances.

I enlisted Rose Gibbons, a marriage family therapist (MFT) and trauma-informed expert, to help me develop and facilitate a live empowerment course for teenage girls, many from Social Services. We called it STARR SuperCamp, and began raising money to fund this innovative healing program.

What we wanted these victimized girls to know was that *they are not what happened to them or in any way responsible for the abuse*. We showed them how to empower themselves through emotional healing work, confidence-building, self-defense training, self-forgiveness, and caring for each other. If I hadn't seen what had happened to my little friend that day and reported it to my mother, who'd taken action, *Martha would have likely suffered a lifetime of abuse*.

My story is that my dad wanted a son, but my mother had four pregnancies, two girls, a son who was stillborn at birth, and ME. Although I know he loved me, on some level I still felt his disappointment. I wanted so much to be his son. I worked very hard at it.

Dad was a hard-working entrepreneur and a builder, among other things, so I studied and got a contractor's license. In California, the test was challenging. The day of my license exam, there were 2,500 taking the test. I was the only woman. I got my license and started a construction company specializing in renovating homes. However, when my dad passed, I still asked myself, *Dad, did I do enough to make you proud?*

I was on a wild ride! I was a mother, contractor, coach, mentor, and employer; a classic "not enough." In my day, I believed boys were more valued than girls. I knew I still had a lot of personal healing to do around this.

In 2008, the country was in a real estate crash. My business and income completely stopped. Although I loved the business, and I had previously experienced much success, I needed to rethink my career. I missed the emotional work I'd been doing with the girls and women. It fulfilled me like nothing else could.

In my sixties, I co-authored *RE—The Wisdom in Rethinking Your Life!* It was written out of my own need to do just that: make a shift. I earned my professional coaching certification and decided to expand the healing work we had done with the girls. Rose and I created a life and leadership course for all women. We called it *Partner in Excellence* (*PIE*). Our book, *RE*, featured short stories of women who had life-changing experiences after participating in PIE. It became an Amazon bestseller in the self-help category.

Just before the pandemic, I started a new Internet program for online coaching. During the lockdowns, we were no longer able to offer in-person courses. This inspired us to write a legacy piece in the form of a guide to memorialize our personal growth work over many decades with girls and women.

The central theme and vision for my courses, books, and healing work has been *Empowered women, empowering women!* I believe empowered women are the tipping point of peace and prosperity in the world today!

I'm grateful to have been invited to participate as an author and share my story for this project, *Voices of the 21st Century: Wise Women Bringing Light to the World*. It is such a beautiful fit given my passion and purpose expressed through my lifelong work and latest book, *The Wisdom Within ME—A Personal Guide for Tapping Into Your Innate SUPERPOWERS*. Together, in our power, we can bring more light to a world that so needs it.

Today, I'm still in construction as a consultant. Frankly, that's where the money is to help support my love of doing this life-changing work.

I've been blessed with many loving relationships: my son, grandsons, son-in-law, ex-husband, and mentors. I'm thankful for my own healing and multiple careers. I'm surrounded by empowered women—my daughter, granddaughter, nieces, clients, and friends—who encourage me to continue this wisdom journey and join other women in bringing light to the world.

May my story inspire you to recognize and unleash your own superpowers.

Gloria Manchester's *coaching career has always focused on empowering women. She has published two books,* RE, *an Amazon bestseller and* The Wisdom Within ME—A Personal Guide for Tapping into Your Innate SUPERPOWERS. *It's an opportunity for women to reflect and listen to their internal WISDOM and unleash their natural SUPERPOWERS.*

CreateAThrivingLifeStory.com

The Wisdom of Trauma

Sheliah J. McDaniel

Life has taught me a lot about resilience and perseverance, none of which, in the moment of the situation, I found pleasant to experience. However, I have found reward in my ability to realize that the stepping stone of every undue and self-inflicted suffering, trauma, heartbreak, and struggle has added to my ability to create a life of success and abundance while adding value to the lives of others.

The stepping stone that laid the foundation for my life's journey began with the trauma of child sexual abuse. I was about four or five years old when my mom and dad decided to divorce. When they separated, we (my mom, three brothers, and me) moved into a family home with two of her siblings and their children. Shortly after, I began to awake in the middle of the night to inappropriate touching and being forced into sexual intercourse. I'm sure some of you reading this are asking the question, "Why didn't you tell someone?" Well, growing up, the family connection ingrained in us was absolutely everything to me. Our family was EXTREMELY close. We were raised in a village of mothers and fathers and sisters and brothers. While I understood the traditional family structure of extended family titles like grandmother, aunt, uncle, and cousin, the love and respect I carried was that of the parent-child and sibling bond. I will be forever grateful for the family values instilled in me, but at the time, that dynamic paralyzed my ability to seek help.

Every time I had the thought to tell my mom about the abuse, I envisioned a world of division and turmoil within my family that felt earth-shattering. What if I can't spend time with my family anymore? What if no one believed me? What if they blamed me? Maybe it was my fault. I must have done something to make him want to do that . . . So many questions and irrational fears constantly plagued me, but at the root of it all was the thought of being "at fault" for tearing our village apart. That was far more debilitating to me than the pain of the trauma I experienced. So, I suffered in silence and did my best to manage the emotions associated with my trauma alone. That trauma set the tone for much of my life's journey. It also lit the fire that has fueled my lifelong drive of perseverance and resilience to give a voice to the voiceless, to seek understanding in the misunderstood, and to lead a life of purpose centered in what I like to call the "Heartcore Leadership."

My ill-equipped attempt to manage my unhealed childhood trauma gifted me the experience of becoming a single mother at the start of my senior year of high school. Since my mother had no knowledge of the trauma I'd experienced, she blamed the challenges I gave her growing up on the fact that my father's presence in my life was nonexistent. She wasn't completely off track, but my "daddy issues" were just fuel on an already out-of-control fire. While I understood that my mom was doing her best with the limited knowledge she had, I often felt harshly judged, greatly misunderstood, and rarely seen. When I got pregnant, part of me desperately wanted someone (anyone) to care enough to dig a little deeper to force out of me what I alone felt incapable of speaking out about on my own. Since I didn't find that in my own experience, I found solace in being that for others.

To me, everyone (regardless of age or position of authority) had the right to feel seen, heard, and understood, but I felt that adults held all the power and influence. The annoyance of that discernment was supported by my mom, allowing me space to speak my mind on areas of disagreement, which seemed to unleash this superpower in me that removed all intimidation associated with addressing those in positions of authority. I held this unshakeable belief that a person's position of authority should not be the driving force behind the value placed on one's voice or influence (sometimes to a fault). To this day, no matter the situation or circumstance, I am unmoved by society's otherwise respect for position and perceived power.

With teenage pregnancy came the narrative that I was defined by my life situation and circumstances. My mother was serving in the U.S. Air Force and deployed overseas, so I had to deliver the unfortunate news of being pregnant to her over the phone. As I think back on this now, as a mother myself, I can only imagine the flood of emotions that came with her loss of control over what was happening with her only daughter. But when she essentially told me I needed to have an abortion because the decision not to do so would ruin every plan I had set for my life, it lit a fire in me to show her, other nay-sayers, and most importantly, my soon-to-be child, that we are not defined by life's seemingly impossible circumstances. I knew, with every sense of my being, that regardless of my current situation, I was going to achieve my goals. I didn't have to choose my life over my son's.

See, I resolved very early that life either happens "to you" or "for you"; it is up to me to determine which is true. In seeing life from the perspective of it happening "for" me, healing and hindsight have given me so many valuable lessons, tools, and gifts, but what lies at the root of it all is the invaluable understanding that life is as good as my mental ability to lead myself and others through it, which is the catalyst of my Heartcore Leadership philosophy: (1) *Everyone has a story deserving of your time to learn*, (2) *No one cares what you know until they know that you care*, and (3) *Everyone deserves to be led well, so start with you.*

Sheliah J. McDaniel *is an executive coach, personal growth strategist, thought leader, and author. She is a purpose-driven strategist who assists individuals and organizations in moving from where they are to where they want to go. Simply put, Sheliah fosters winning solutions through the power of authentic and purpose-driven leadership.*

SheliahMcDaniel.com

THE POWER WITHIN HER STORY

Amber Mesorana

It was Easter weekend, a time for joy and family bonding. We spent it at a beachside resort with friends. The weather was perfect, the sun was bright over the ocean, and the air was filled with children's laughter. It felt like the ideal getaway.

We basked in the sun's warmth, building sandcastles and collecting seashells. The ocean waves lapped gently against the shore, and the smell of saltwater mingled with that of the barbecues. Little did we know the idyllic day would soon take a tragic turn, forever altering our lives.

The day was winding down as we reluctantly packed our belongings, ready to return to the beach house. We took the golf cart back, and my husband, who had been cheerful all day, collapsed once we got to our room on the house's third floor. Panic set in as I realized something was wrong. My world was turned upside down.

I watched in horror as friends, family, and paramedics worked frantically to save him. Time seemed to stretch and blur. Despite their best efforts, my husband passed away that day from a heart attack, leaving a gaping void in our lives.

The days that followed were a blur of grief, disbelief, and overwhelming sadness. Losing my husband so suddenly and unexpectedly was a shock, and I found myself grappling with a whirlwind of emotions. It wasn't just the immediate loss that I had to deal with—his death unearthed long-buried feelings and unresolved issues from my past.

As I began the journey of healing, I realized this tragedy had opened old wounds I had ignored for years. My coping mechanism had always been to suppress my emotions and keep moving forward, but I couldn't run from them anymore.

Recognizing that I couldn't navigate this path alone, I turned to therapy. In these sessions, I began to unravel the complex layers of my grief and pain. Therapy taught me that true healing requires confronting and processing emotions rather than burying them.

I learned that my tendency to ignore my feelings had only caused them to fester, triggering painful memories and reactions. The therapy sessions were grueling but illuminating, showing me the importance of addressing my past to move forward.

Through therapy, I embarked on a journey of self-discovery. I began to understand the root causes of my emotional struggles and how my childhood experiences had shaped my coping mechanisms. It was a painful process but also a liberating one. I started to see myself more clearly, recognizing my strength and resilience.

I realized that throughout my life, I had been looking for someone to save me, to help me navigate my struggles, but now, I understood that I was the only person who could save me. This realization was both daunting and empowering.

While devastating, my husband's death was the catalyst for my transformation, forcing me to confront unresolved issues and take responsibility for my healing. It was a turning point, a new chapter in my life.

I began to practice self-compassion, giving myself the grace to grieve and heal at my own pace. I learned to acknowledge my emotions without judgment, understanding that they were a natural part of my healing journey.

As I continued to work on myself, I saw changes in my life. I became more mindful and present, no longer running from my emotions but facing them head-on. I developed healthier coping mechanisms and built a support system of friends and family who understood and supported my journey.

I also rediscovered my passions and interests and found joy in small things I had previously overlooked. This newfound sense of purpose and fulfillment was a testament to my progress.

Throughout this process, I discovered a strength within myself I never knew existed. I realized that I had always been strong, even in my moments of weakness. My husband's death had stripped away the layers of fear and insecurity, revealing the resilient person underneath.

I learned that healing is not a linear process. It has its ups and downs and its moments of clarity and confusion, but through it all, I remained committed to my journey, understanding that every step forward was a victory, no matter how small.

As I reflect on this journey, I am grateful for the lessons I learned and the growth I experienced. My husband's death was a heartbreaking event, but it also brought me back to my true self, helping me heal and find peace.

I know the road ahead will continue to have its challenges, but I am confident in my ability to navigate them. I have learned to trust myself, to listen to my inner voice, and to embrace the journey, knowing I have the strength to overcome whatever comes my way.

This chapter of my life marks a new beginning filled with hope, resilience, and self-love. I am no longer looking for someone to save me because I have found strength within myself. My journey of healing and self-discovery is ongoing, but I am ready to face it with an open heart and a renewed sense of purpose.

Throughout this process, I have learned that true healing comes from within. It requires courage, vulnerability, and a willingness to confront our deepest fears and pains, but it also brings a profound sense of freedom and empowerment, allowing us to live more fully and authentically.

My story is one of loss and grief but also of healing and transformation. It is a testament to the resilience of the human spirit and the power of self-love. As I continue this journey, I am reminded that I can overcome any obstacle and that the strength I need is already within me. It has always been within me.

In the face of unimaginable loss, I found myself. I found a path to healing and a way to honor my husband's memory by living a life filled with purpose and love, and for that, I am eternally grateful.

Amber Mesorana's journey exemplifies resilience and strength. After losing her husband, she discovered her inner power and reshaped her life. As founder of The Power of Her Story, Amber inspires women to unlock their potential within their own stories, navigate challenges with grace, and emerge stronger. Her mission empowers women to thrive.

AmberMesorana.com

DE-CLOAKING TO SHINE MY OWN LIGHT

Jennifer Mitchell

I used to hold on to my corporate identity like a tailored suit—not that we were wearing tailored suits to the office anymore—and I was bridging two opposing worlds. By day, I was known for leading high-value, cutting-edge projects, from developing project teams to implementing new technologies and creating customer value. By night, it was as though I had a non-paying side hustle: I was literally sent to see people who had passed and guide them to the light, similar to a medium.

This is a story of "de-cloaking," of how I lifted off the corporate identity to acknowledge that mediumship was a gift, and how I transformed my passion for mediumship into a thriving business that has a positive impact in both the business and spiritual realms.

For a very long time, I hid that I was intuitive and my ability to hear messages from the "other side." For me, mediumship is about listening to guidance, which informs my intuition. I started small, using intuition to gauge the sincerity of potential business partners or the timing of important decisions. In meetings, I could sense the energy in the room shifting and was able to facilitate better outcomes. In transformation projects, I could visualize an entire structure and intuitively piece together the puzzle to see missed links and connections.

The decision to de-cloak—to fully embrace and reveal my gift of mediumship—was not easy. It took a lot of courage to step away from a stable, respected career and tip-toe into a whole new business model. In fact, some friends and colleagues of twenty-plus years are only now finding out. As soon as I did, my gifts expanded. It was like having a team of virtual assistants on hand, guiding me with the next steps and passing me information—shame they don't do the admin as well!

With practice, I honed connecting with spirit and channeling messages. I realized my unique abilities provided comfort to grieving loved ones. The messages I received from their passed loved (or not-so-loved) ones cleared blocks and old beliefs in an instant. I also incorporated ancestral healing, helping clients break free from inherited limitations and embrace their fullest potential. To my amazement, I can even channel information from prominent figures, such as Steve Jobs, on creating innovative solutions. I've empowered myself, my friends, and my clients to transform our lives and live in alignment with our true selves.

The fulfillment I found through mediumship and coaching was unmatched by anything in my corporate career. I loved the corporate project work—finding solutions, successes, and outcomes—but it often came at the personal cost of forcing change. I've merged my two worlds by integrating intuition and mediumship into consulting, executive coaching, and speaking, creating a fun business and greater success in all aspects of my life.

Although this has been a de-cloaking, it has come full circle to be integrated in three important aspects. For corporations, I envision a future where intuition is seamlessly integrated into business decision-making alongside data analytics for a holistic approach to leadership and strategy. Intuitive insights, often overlooked in traditional corporate settings, can complement empirical data, leading to more comprehensive and adaptive decision-making. For businesses, embracing intuition means recognizing the value of human insight and experience, fostering a culture of creativity, empathy, and visionary thinking.

Equally important is the role of healers and spiritual coaches in this integration. By helping individuals connect with their inner wisdom and live authentically, these practitioners cultivate a workforce that is more engaged and purpose-driven. When employees feel supported in their personal growth and can bring their whole selves to work, the result is a more productive and innovative workforce.

Thirdly, this future offers an expanded influence and often improved business structure for those in the healing and spiritual fields. By bridging the gap between the "mystical" and the practical, healers can demystify intuition, making it accessible to a broader audience and fostering a balanced, insightful, and enlightened approach to achieving organizational and personal goals.

A pivotal part of my de-cloaking journey has been the stripping away of perceived societal expectations and self-imposed limits to reveal my true self. In the corporate world, I often wore a mask, conforming to what I thought was expected, but as I delved deeper into my spiritual practice, I realized the power of authenticity. De-cloaking has allowed me to present my whole self, fostering deeper connections and more meaningful interactions. By fusing my professional skills with my spiritual gifts, I've created a fulfilling, purpose-driven life. By magnifying my light, I've contributed to the brilliance of the whole, inspiring others to seek higher understanding and live in their own light.

I bridge the material and spiritual worlds to encourage my clients to listen to their inner guidance, pursue their passions, and, most importantly, trust in their power to create meaningful change in their lives. One of my clients, a high-powered lawyer who now meditates and embraces his intuition, shared how he reconnected with his late mother during a meditation. "For years, I've been driven by a need to prove myself, but I'd lost sight of who I am. Thank you for helping me find my way to me," he said.

In truth, my clients have helped me find my way to myself.

This reciprocal growth shows the power of integrating our professional and spiritual selves. We unlock our full potentials, leading to a richer, more vibrant existence. The key to such integration is authenticity and self-awareness. By staying true to our essences and embracing our unique paths, we inspire others to do the same. True de-cloaking.

My experience underscores the transformative power of following my inner voice. Living a purpose-driven life where the professional and spiritual coexist harmoniously empowers me to shine brightly and encourage others on their own transformative journeys.

Jennifer Mitchell*, a twenty-five-year leader in corporate transformation, embraced her mediumship gift to empower others. She integrates intuition with consulting, coaching, and speaking to support clients to achieve their fullest potentials. Jennifer's unique journey blends professional expertise with spiritual insight, helping people achieve abundance in relationships, work, and life.*

JenniferMitchell.me

I Found My Birth Father

Fonda Neal

I grew up with the belief that my father had passed away when I was a baby. Whenever I had to fill out paperwork for school or at a doctor's office, I would automatically write "deceased" in the father section of the form. My mom never talked to me about my dad, ever. I did not even know his name.

As I grew older, especially around the time I reached junior high school, my curiosity about my father began to intensify. One day, I gathered the courage to ask my oldest sister, who was quite knowledgeable about our family's history, if she knew anything about my father, what his name was, and so on. She did not know anything but encouraged me to ask our mother about him. I was apprehensive at first because, after all, it was a sensitive subject. Shortly after that conversation with my sister, I developed enough courage to ask my mother about my dad. I asked her what his name was, how she'd met him, and what he looked like. To my surprise, she answered my questions without hesitation. She told me that he looked just like me, that he was tall, and that they had met at the military base near where we lived. She also told me his first and last name. However, she didn't know much else about him. She explained that she hadn't asked him many questions and that shortly after I was born, he had been transferred from the military base in Virginia to another location out of state.

At the age of fifteen, I decided to embark on a journey to find my father. My first step was writing to the *Oprah Winfrey Show*. In the late '80s, Oprah was known for reuniting families and helping people find their loved ones, so I thought if anyone could help me find my father, it was Oprah! I received a postcard in the mail from Harpo Studios acknowledging my letter, but, unfortunately, nothing more came of it. Undeterred, I continued my search into the early '90s with the help of a book I purchased on how to find anyone anywhere.

I wrote to the Army Military Personnel Center, providing them with all the information I had: his name (spelled the way it sounded to me when my mother told me his name: last name of Michael), my birth date, and the name of the local military base where he was stationed at the time of my birth. I received a response back by mail indicating they were unable to identify a record of military service based on the information I provided. This was a setback, but it didn't deter me.

Many years passed, but I never gave up on my desire to find my father. I longed to know if he was actually deceased or if there was a chance he was still alive. I had so many unanswered questions: Did he know I existed? Why had he left? Did he have other children?

Fast forward to 2018, when my husband encouraged me to register with 23andMe, a genetic testing service, to see if there might be any matches. I felt it was a long shot, but I submitted my 23andMe kit. The immediate results did not reveal any close matches, which was disappointing. Periodically, I received emails from 23andMe, notifying me of new DNA relatives to view. I would log in to look sometimes, but many times, I ignored the emails, thinking I would be disappointed again because there would be no strong matches.

In early 2021, I was having a conversation with a close friend from high school about her heritage. She shared her 23andMe results, which prompted me to log into my 23andMe account to take a look at my heritage. When I saw that I had a 7% match, my heart dropped, and I was filled with anticipation! I'd matched with a person whose last name sounded like my father's last name, although it was spelled differently than I had been spelling it in my search for him. Excitedly, I googled the name using the spelling that I saw in my 23andMe profile. To my astonishment, my father's name appeared in the search results, along with an address and a phone number! I don't think I have ever been that excited or nervous to make a phone call in my entire life! On my third attempt to call, I reached someone who turned out to be my father's wife. She answered all of the questions I asked her affirmatively. She was incredibly kind, understanding, supportive, and just a pleasure to talk to. To learn that I had finally found my father and that he was alive was one of the best days of my life, second only to giving birth to my son.

In August 2021, despite the ongoing pandemic, my family and I flew to Georgia so I could meet my father in person. This was definitely a highlight for me during such a devastating time in the world. The week I spent with him, my stepmom, and my newfound siblings was nothing short of amazing. It was surreal to finally connect with the man I had been searching for almost my entire life.

While it may be impossible to make up for fifty-three lost years, I am still enjoying sharing the love for my father and my paternal family through many, many phone calls, Facetime sessions, text messages, the exchange of pictures, and as many in-person visits as possible. What if I had given up? What if I had not remained faithful and steadfast? This experience has taught me the true value of perseverance, patience, and faithfulness. It's a testament to the importance of never giving up on the desires of your heart.

***Fonda Neal** is a higher education professional, author and natural health practitioner whose passion is to inspire and educate health-conscious adults in using natural approaches to wellness. As a neurodivergent individual with ADHD, OCPD, Misophonia and fragrance sensitivities, she is a huge advocate for greater awareness and understanding of invisible disabilities.*

FondaNealNaturalHealth.com

Beyond Belief: How Actions Manifest Miracles

Kashaun Parker

"If one of you says to them, 'Go in peace; keep warm and well fed,' but does nothing about their physical needs, what good is it? In the same way, faith by itself if it is not accompanied by action, is dead."—James 2:16–17

Life is unpredictable in every sense of the word. I think that when we wish and hope for easy, we lose sight of all we can create through action by faith. When I step up to do what is possible, God steps in and does what is impossible.

Senior year of high school was a dream I had nurtured since freshman year. I envisioned it filled with excitement, from Homecoming and Prom to finally walking across the stage at graduation. That year was particularly special because I started dating my first serious boyfriend over the summer. We began the year strong, and I felt on top of the world, balancing honors courses and staying on the honor roll, but just as the year was winding down and we were preparing for college entrance exams, everything changed. I received an unexpected call from my boyfriend, who sounded unusually curt and agitated, but I dismissed it as stress from our busy schedules.

"Hey, babe—what's going on with you today?" I asked.

"Nothing. So, you making it a habit to be rude to people now?" he retorted.

Confused, I asked what he meant, but he abruptly ended the call. Then, I recalled an exchange I'd had with a girl at school earlier that day about her interactions with my boyfriend. I was preparing to call him back to explain when there was a knock at my door. It was my cousin, saying I had a visitor. It was my boyfriend's cousin, who handed me a handwritten note before leaving. The note revealed that my boyfriend was breaking up with me, saying we were too different, and he couldn't continue.

Devastated, I tried to keep moving forward, but my grades plummeted, and I barely slept or ate. I was a mess. This pattern went on for months. I fell into a terrible depression, and my anxiety was at an all-time high.

I dozed off in my accounting class one day, only to be jolted awake by Mr. S, my teacher, banging on the desk next to me. "You sleep at home, Ms. Hughes, not in my class. Stick around after. I want to talk," he said.

After class, he looked at me with concern. "What upsets me is that you have so much potential, and you're throwing it away. God helps those who help themselves. I know you're hurting, but you can't just quit."

His words struck a chord. I recognized it as a pep talk, though I didn't fully grasp the full meaning then. He was right! At just eighteen, I'd faced significant challenges, yet I had so much more to give. Despite everything I'd endured, quitting would have rendered it all meaningless. I couldn't give in. I pulled myself together, graduated, and went on to college. Mr. S's message, especially when he'd said, "God helps those who help themselves" stayed with me and fueled my determination. Whenever I hear someone say, "I'm waiting on God," I think of Mr. S's words. They have resonated with me deeply and shaped my understanding of faith and action.

I've learned that God often shows up in unexpected ways, but they usually require us to take that first step in faith. It's a lesson I've seen play out in my lifetime, again and again. The book of James teaches that faith without works is dead. Simply believing isn't enough; we must take action, even when it's hard, and that's when God's miracles unfold.

Consider the countless stories of divine intervention. Rarely do miracles happen in a vacuum. More often, they occur after someone takes a bold step despite uncertainty and fear. It's in these moments of courage and determination that God's power is most evident.

In my own journey, there have been numerous instances where I've found myself at a crossroads, pleading for God to intervene, from the loss of my parents to the loss of my husband, and even while navigating a complete career change. All of my miracles started with me taking the first step by faith.

It wasn't until I'd mustered the courage to take action on that first uncertain step that I witnessed profound changes. Whether it was starting a new venture or overcoming personal challenges, the principle remained the same: action ignites faith, and faith invites miracles.

This principle extends beyond personal experience. In the broader scope of our communities and society, the most significant changes often start with individuals taking initiative. When we step up to address a need, solve a problem, or support others, we become vessels through which God's work is accomplished.

Faith is not passive. It is an active, dynamic force that propels us forward, even when the path is unclear. It requires us to trust in God's plan and take responsibility for our actions. In doing so, we create opportunities for growth, transformation, and the manifestation of divine assistance.

Mr. S's message serves as a constant reminder that I have a role to play in my destiny. It's a call to action, urging me to rise above adversity and pursue my goals with determination and faith. By helping ourselves, we open the door for God's grace to enter our lives and work wonders we never could have imagined.

Whenever I face a seemingly insurmountable obstacle, I remember that waiting passively isn't the answer. Instead, I take a step forward, confident God will meet me along the way to guide and support me as I move toward my dreams.

Mr. S's advice has become foundational in my life. It has guided me through challenges and triumphs, reminding me that faith and action together create the path to success because God helps those who help themselves.

Kashaun Parker *is a keynote speaker, bestselling author, and business strategist. She empowers entrepreneurs with strategies for business development and resilience. As a passionate advocate for entrepreneurship, Kashaun helps clients reduce stress and achieve sustainable growth. She is the founder of Next Step Forward and a dedicated mother of three.*

NextStepForwardCoach.com

Laurel's Own Words

Laurel Anda Charlong Penner

In "Laurel's Own Words," we are invited into the heart of a remarkable journey. Through her diary, Laurel shares her raw, unfiltered conversations with God, revealing a profound trust and surrender. Her words—a legacy of faith, courage, and an unwavering belief in the power of grace—inspire us to embrace each moment with gratitude and hope.

Lord, I am afraid of totally giving myself over to You because I am afraid of what I will become.

God, this journey You are taking me on, I need Your help every second. I don't want to muster the strength on my own. I don't have any. God, where are You taking me?

Life's experiences should bring about growth in one's character and spiritual life, like the character development in the movie *Risen*, to seek out truth and then act on it.

We all have events, situations, or circumstances thrown at us. My encouragement would be to let go of things that need to be gone from your life, like the hurt, the differences, and the judgment. I don't want to be the same. I asked Dan (my husband) to promise me no more "Kumbyya," never be the same; we all must be open to change.

I am physically and mentally tired. I am weary. Very weary. Thank You for Your strength. I am grateful You are with me at all times. Thank You for sustaining me. I know this is only day-by-day, and I am learning how important that really is. It gives me such clarity because I have no strength, so each day, I have to meet with You. That desire comes from You, God. I love You. You have told me to trust You completely, so with Your strength, I say, YES. Thank You for Your power and presence.

Thank You for going before me (Deut 31:8), for being with me, and for never leaving nor forsaking me. I am not to fear or be discouraged, so in Your name, I will not.

God, breathe Your wisdom over me so I can understand You; Your decisions, Your testing, have taught me what is true and right. Oh, love me now. Hold me the way You have promised.

God, give me grace to walk humbly before You. We are all given these moments to hold in our hands, and they are as sand sifting through our fingers. Yesterday is gone, and tomorrow may never come, but we have this moment. We have today.

I don't know what today will bring, but You do, Lord. Much stress comes from wanting to make things happen before their time. The way forward is moment by moment, and I will wait as long as God says. Everything I had hoped for comes from Him, and why not? He is rock solid and under my feet. He is breath for my soul. He is my safe harbor, so I will trust Him absolutely. My strength comes from Him, and I will hold onto that. He is at my side. He is encouraging me, carrying me. He leads me in peace. He is my future, my hope, and my song, and I will hold His hand.

I don't know about tomorrow; I just live day to day. I am going to the river, Lord, meet me there. I am ready to surrender. Jesus, You long to meet me there. Take my hand; my life beyond compare.

Lord, You hid me away. You provided an escape, a tranquil space. The home I had, the acreage—I was hidden away in beauty. You keep moving quietly, softly. Nothing phases You or is a surprise to You. You are in control. All of nature is under it. Spring happens, blossoms, gardens, new life emerges. What is it that attracts me to forests, mountains, oceans, streams and meadows, snow-covered landscapes, sunrises and sunsets, the moon and the stars? It all shouts Your peace and Your majesty. It shows Your glory. Its unity shows me that You pull me together. You protect my heart and my mind, and You assure me that You are right here for me.

You mentor me far from my troubles. I have nothing to fear. Terror can't even come close to me. You will see to it that everything works out for the best. I will focus my eyes on the eternal.

Here I am, a full life and in the emptiest of places. If one gets rid of prejudices, quits blaming and being a victim, quits gossiping, if you are generous and giving of yourself, your life will begin to glow in the darkness. Your shadowed life will be bathed in sunlight. You will know where to go. Be thankful for blessings and love. Show grace, have mercy, and be kind. Be a witness of Christ so you can relate to others. Then, you will have a full life in the emptiest of places.

I have no power over my life except that which God gives me; I have power over my thoughts and my actions. Thankfulness lifts me above my circumstances.

Lord, Your beauty and love chase after me every day of my life.

I want to look death in the face and not flinch. You embrace me. You are company to the lowest, and Your cause is to the black sheep. I will not be embarrassed because You have forgotten all of my humiliations. It is with lasting love that You, Lord, tenderly care for me. You will not walk away from me.

Suffering brings about growth. God's work is woven out of pain. This is hard, discouraging, so crushing. The pain overwhelms me. The onslaught of bad news is unbelievable. Every morning is a choice to stay on course, to trust You inexplicably, not to allow discouragement to set in.

The power of worship daily, continually, the power of casting my cares, hurt, and anxieties on Christ today, knowing God will give me strength again for tomorrow.

What does victory look like for me? What can I expect? What am I to do? I need You.

I love You, God, and I have done my best.

Laurel Anda Charlong Penner *was an elite athlete whose dedication and discipline on the field were matched only by her love for her family. A devoted mother and wife, she cherished her moments with her two sons, her husband, and her family and friends. Her legacy is one of resilience, love, and unwavering commitment to those she held dear. Laurel passed away gracefully on December 7, 2022, after a five-month journey with cancer.*

WHEN LIFE THROWS YOU LEMONS . . .

Rachel Pietsch

Shortly after my husband and I returned home to Australia after living in Canada for nine months in 2006, we realized he was suffering from professional burnout. We had intended to stay in Toronto for a couple of years, but the work environment he endured was toxic and soul-crushing, and because our visas were dependent on his job, we had to return to Melbourne. This marked the beginning of the hardest three years of my life.

Firstly, I wasn't the main breadwinner. My husband is a highly intelligent engineer who always excelled in whatever he did. Having been raised in a Fundamentalist Christian household where women were taught to defer to men, be it their father or husband, I believed it was my husband's responsibility to be the main provider. I did have a teaching degree, but I never considered myself a "career woman."

It took me about a year to fully accept what my husband was going through. Initially, I thought he just needed a break for a few months before getting back to work, but looking for jobs was becoming increasingly stressful for him. Before long, I could see he was falling deeper into anxiety and depression. Getting back on track was going to take longer than a few months, so I needed to give hubby space, time in therapy, and step up. After all, we had a mortgage to pay.

I took any job I could find—retail, my parents' dry cleaners, and relief teaching, which I knew I loathed after having taught for three years in various schools in my early career—and prepared to endure it to keep a roof over our heads. This was an incredibly tumultuous time. I was so scared. I was used to the significant people in my life doing most of the "adulting" for me. There were so many unknowns, and apart from feeling a great deal of pressure to make ends meet, I also witnessed a significant shift in the man I love that I couldn't comprehend. I was quickly losing hope of us finding a way back to the life we had before, and I had no idea what it was going to look like moving forward. Little did I know I was about to begin my own incredible, life-altering journey.

It was a weekday afternoon in those early months. I was relief-teaching at a school I had previously worked at, and I had just sent a grade five class back to their classroom after their drama session. At the end of the school day, I was relieved I didn't have to subject myself to more feelings of failure as a teacher; it was a far too familiar sentiment I'd felt since the beginning of my classroom teaching career, leaving me drained and confused. I knew I loved teaching, but why did I still feel as if I couldn't connect with my students? I didn't feel capable of holding their attention or imparting anything truly significant.

I remember as I was packing up, another teacher came into the room and began setting up for her drama class the next morning. She was bustling around the room, humming as she went, with a bounce in her step. I didn't get it. What was it about the job that could possibly make you hum and bounce, especially at the end of the day? So, I said to her with an edge of desperation, "I don't know how you do this job. What keeps you going?" Her reply was what changed my course forever.

She said, "This job energizes me."

Boom! That one statement cut right through every feeling of inadequacy and frustration I had been carrying. Something big shifted, and all of a sudden, I sensed a different path. It was as if I were standing there, looking at the yellow brick road or a stairway to heaven. The heaviness in my body just lifted as it dawned on me: classroom teaching absolutely did not energize me. Blessed relief! I didn't care if I was wasting my degree—I had found the permission to walk away.

But how was I going to keep the money we desperately needed coming in?

I happened to have a backup solution, which I'd not seriously considered as it involved working for myself and would take time to build a decent income. You see, the reason I knew I loved teaching was because I had already done it in a private capacity in my final year of high school and all through university. I taught piano and voice, which were also my majors as a part of my classroom music teaching degree.

I pursued my degree because of my passion for private teaching, so returning to it felt like a natural choice.

I knew I had chosen the right path as soon as I began. Yes, funds were even tighter, but I was happier. Working with one person at a time allowed me to deliver a better quality service tailored for each person. I became more curious about my craft, seeking out further training and building my confidence. I began to develop opinions and beliefs that were different from those of my upbringing, which helped me connect more with different people and the world around me. You could say that despite the tough times, I was finding myself.

At first, I thought I would eventually take a step back when my husband was well enough to work again, but I never did. I had found my purpose, and I was building something that fulfilled me. I was beginning to understand where grit, tenacity, and self-belief could take me, and I can now proudly say that I built a thriving, award-winning business helping people find their voice.

I can say that when I chose to be brave, I flourished, and I can truly say that, at the end of every day, I feel energized.

***Rachel Pietsch** is a multi-award-winning vocal coach who has been teaching voice for over thirty years and is accredited in voice function. She works with the mechanics of the voice, bringing better ease, projection, and longevity to both speakers and singers, helping them elevate their careers and impact.*

NowYoureTalking.com.au

Journey to Self: Unveiling My Authentic Identity

Valerie Priester

Can you picture this: a sweet little girl, no more than seven or eight, teaching her Barbie dolls how to live their best lives? She had them all lined up on the couch, a ruler in her hand, pointing to lessons on her little chalkboard. That little girl was me. Yes, even at that tender age, I felt an undeniable desire to teach. My dolls, about six or seven of them, became my students. I can't recall the specifics of what I taught them, but in my heart, I remember it as earth-shattering knowledge about how to be, do, and have whatever they desired.

Little did I know this childhood game would foreshadow my life decades later. Today, I'm not a teacher in the traditional sense, but I am a teacher of life strategies, guiding women to create abundant lives. When people ask how I started my career as a mindset coach, this is the story I share. It took many years for me to connect the dots, but that little girl teaching her dolls is a big part of who I am today.

The journey to becoming the woman I am today was far from a straight line. Every step, every experience, was a piece of the puzzle. My journey began with a decision: a decision that I deserved God's best. This was the major turning point, the decision that set me on the path to where I am now. Along this path, I faced heartbreak, disappointment, challenges, struggles, and broken dreams. Each of these experiences taught me invaluable lessons and profound wisdom.

I often think about the advice and wisdom I would give that little girl who had once taught her dolls. I am so grateful I get to share it with you in this book.

The first lesson I learned was to discover who I am. So many well-meaning people in my life tried to tell me who I was or what I was meant to be. While they had my best interests at heart, no one can tell us who we are. That's a personal journey for each of us. I started this journey of discovery by reflecting on my life. I'm almost ashamed to say I was well into my thirties when I started this journey, although I believe it takes time for us to come to that moment when we see the need to dig deeper into discovering who we are. Life before this, for me, was mostly about survival.

Next, I had to define what I wanted in this life. For years, I went in circles, trying to decide and define my desires. There were many options, but I learned that the only true option for me was the one that made my heart sing: helping other women be their best and create meaningful lives. This was not a speedy decision. It took me a few years of trying several paths. I learned to practice sitting in silence so I could hear what my heart was saying to me. I heard it loud and clear: my true calling was helping others.

One of the hardest lessons was believing in myself. Raised by my grandparents, I had an abundance of love but very little encouragement. I attribute this to the generational gap. Being a grandmother now, I understand that raising a small child while in their later years had to have been challenging. This did not help my self-belief, which I had to develop on my own. I kept a "Success" journal, documenting all my accomplishments. This helped remind me that I am full of greatness. A strong self-belief fuels your courage to take risks, pursue ambitious goals, and navigate challenges with resilience.

Another difficult lesson was recognizing and acknowledging my worth. As I embarked on my career as a coach, I dealt with imposter syndrome. It was strange because I could see the impact my coaching had on others, helping them improve their lives and businesses, but I had trouble acknowledging it for myself. Often, we discard our gifts as things everyone should know how to do. However, our gifts are unique to us, and with them, we bring our true worth into the world.

Love—ah, the lessons around love were also challenging. When we struggle with loving ourselves, it becomes difficult to give and receive love. Learning to love myself transformed my personal and professional life. Personally, it helped me be a better woman in all my relationships, especially in attracting my amazing husband. Professionally, it made me a better coach, allowing me to have compassion and empathy for my clients and teaching them to love themselves on their journeys.

A very valuable lesson for me was developing a positive growth mindset. For years, I struggled with a scarcity mindset, thinking I would never have enough to take care of myself and my daughter. As a single mother, life wasn't always easy. I had a lot of support from my family, but I wanted to be self-sufficient. Shifting my mindset was and still is a journey. As a mindset coach, it has been my life's work to develop a mindset that allows me to be authentic and completely whole in what I teach. Some of the techniques I use to shift my mindset are creating positive affirmations, listening to positive messages, reading books on abundance mindset, journaling, and reviewing my client testimonials. I also have a daily ritual of meditation and visualizing what I want. These practices help retrain my subconscious mind to believe that all things are possible.

As your partner in designing your victory, I hope the lessons I've shared will help you create a victorious, abundant, and well-balanced life. The journey isn't always easy, but every step, every lesson, brings you closer to living your best life. Embrace the journey, believe in yourself, and know that you deserve all the abundance life has to offer.

Valerie Priester is a master mindset coach, best-selling author, and motivational speaker. She is CEO of Victorious Life Coaching, where she offers comprehensive coaching services covering mindset, business, money mastery, and personal development. Her mission in life is to empower women to lead victorious lives filled with success and fulfillment.

ValeriePriester.com

Never Waste a Crisis

Meng Quah-Shepherd

It was in March 2006. My sister, a doctor, called to say she had my mammogram results. Could I swing by for dinner to discuss?

Have you ever had a gut feeling that something was terribly wrong?

That evening, she gave me the news that I had breast cancer. My immediate reaction was to wonder if I was going to die. I sat in her stairwell and cried quietly. Even as I write this now, I feel the tears build up in my eyes. I had just been through a sinister divorce—a story for another time. It had left me emotionally and psychologically depleted and alone, as does the aftermath of most divorces. Those of you who have been through one—I share your pain.

So, having the news of breast cancer was like having fallen off a cliff and climbed back up only to be pushed off the cliff again, not knowing if I would survive this time.

My treatment involved surgery and radiotherapy. I was one of the lucky ones not in need of chemotherapy. My journey after surgery was life-changing in that I learned many lessons, which I now share in the hope they will help others.

How was breast cancer a blessing for me?

After surgery, I rested for a week. I did not feel unwell, so I went back to work. I am a dentist and a business owner. I forgot how much tension is placed on my upper body in my work and the stitches I had all split. I was horrified. What had I done? Luckily, the surgeon reassured me the damage was minimal, but now I would have a large scar.

Lesson: feeling okay does not mean your body has fully healed.

I then had to start radiotherapy sessions several times a week. I maneuvered these sessions into my patient schedule. I thought I had my time management perfectly nailed!

Then, a miracle happened in the sense that an *angel* was sent to me. One day, as I was running back to my car after the radiotherapy, the receptionist called out to me, saying, "Meng, may I have a quick word? It's important."

She sat me down with a glass of water and calmly said, "I have been watching you for a couple of weeks now, and I see you fly in here and fly out with a sandwich in hand."

I thought, *So, what is your point?* She looked me in the eye and said, "I don't think you have accepted what has happened to you. You have cancer, and you need to look after you. Now is your time, and it is about you."

This was unbelievable. It was almost as if someone had taken a rock off my chest. In spending my life building my business and trying to please everyone, *I had lost myself.*

That day, as I drove home after surgery, I could not stop the tears because I realized how physically and mentally tired I really was. It had taken a stranger to bring me to my senses.

Lesson: the universe is here to look after us if we open our minds, stop, and listen.

Another amazing experience happened. I learned to listen to my body more, and I felt the call to do yoga, so I called around, looking for a private teacher. I rang a lady just down the road from me. She quite abruptly informed me that she did not do personal classes. I left my number with her in case she thought of someone. She rang me the next day to say she had changed her mind and would teach me. Weeks later, she said she had a dream about me the night I'd first called. In the dream, she was told to help me. She was amazed at how I took to yoga like fish to water in my first lesson. Was that a spiritual experience?

So, how was having breast cancer a life-changer? Being the youngest child, I'd always felt my sisters were smarter than me. I learned to please everyone, say yes, and agree to everything. I had no idea what I should do for myself and what I should allow others to ask of me.

I had gone to boarding school in the UK, where I had no family. I got married and moved to Australia because my husband at the time wanted to do so, and my sister encouraged me to go where my family was. All of my decisions had been heavily influenced by what others thought.

Having breast cancer gave me many lessons that were life-changing:
1. It is okay to stop and smell the roses.

2. Life throws you the good and bad. No matter what, the universe looks after us, and there are great people out there who will reach out to us; you are not alone.
3. Be fearless, no matter what. We are all *LIFE WARRIORS*, but always remember that without good health, life is more of a challenge.

Today, my life is rich, with great people and yoga. I even took up competitive dragon boating, having never considered myself to be athletic before. The dragon boat team, Dragons Abreast Sydney, is made up of an awesome bunch of breast cancer survivors who have the attitude that no mountain is too high to climb.

I schedule in **ME TIME**.

I encourage you all to embrace life, listen to your bodies, and schedule self-care time.

You are the architect of your life. Only you can design the life you desire.

Meng Quah-Shepherd is a cosmetic dentist. Founder of Boutique Dental Care Chatswood, she creates life-changing smiles that add confidence and build careers for those seeking her expertise. She has successfully created an atmosphere in her practice that diminishes the challenges and anxiety people have regarding their dental care.

BoutiqueDentalCare.com.au

Breaking the Chains: A Tale of Resilience, Rebellion, and Rebirth

Alexandra X. Quinn

At the tender age of two, it is said that most children go through the "terrible twos," but for me, it was an ordeal far beyond the mere label of "terrible"; it was downright horrific.

At two years old, your entire world revolves around your parents. They are your anchors, your protectors, your everything, but growing up in the grips of poverty in China, that sense of security was tragically snatched from me. My parents had to make an agonizing decision to leave me to be cared for by my grandparents and seek work in distant cities.

I lived in the rural outskirts. I saw my parents a couple of times a year at best. For a child, that absence felt like an eternity. I would gaze up at passing airplanes and call out, "Please, bring back my parents," but the planes came and went, leaving me yearning more for their return. From then on, over and over again, I told myself that I was not even good enough to live with my parents, and a sense of abandonment overcast my early childhood.

Thankfully, my mother's parents stepped in with kindness, helping me navigate this unfamiliar terrain. Yet even in their care, I couldn't escape the harsh realities of that society, where the one-child policy loomed large. Being born a girl was seen as a mark of shame because I was regarded as insufficient to carry on the family name and lineage.

It's difficult for us to understand such injustices in this modern world, but for my family, it was a reality not too long ago. Even today, my father, who is in his seventies, still lives with the guilt of not having a son to fulfill his duty as a firstborn son in his family.

Through the lens of my childhood, I witnessed the stark disparities and endured the painful consequences of societal norms that a woman's worth is based solely on her ability to give birth to a son. I sacrificed playtime and pushed myself to study hard to prove to my father that I could do better than a boy. I programmed myself to do exactly what my parents wanted me to do in the hope I would be accepted as a "good girl."

I learned to suppress my feelings and desires in order to avoid physical punishment from my father and the possibility of being abandoned again, yet without these experiences, I would not be the person I am today. I learned to discipline myself to study, to be resilient, and to survive in harsh environments where women were deemed unworthy. I learned to be grateful for every opportunity that showed up in my life. I even learned to speak English to express myself in a language my parents couldn't understand, which led to an opportunity to study in Europe and my later immigration to Australia.

I am forever grateful for my strict parents, who pushed me to check all the boxes of traditional success. I have dual degrees in Arts and Business, a master's in Accounting, a CPA, prestigious stints at big-four accounting firms, and a promising banking career. I also have a beautiful family with two kids and a loving husband; my life seemed like a portrait of fulfillment.

One day, my nine-year-old daughter asked me a question at playtime. She said, "Mummy, you always asked us to dream big and achieve high, so what is your dream?" No words came to my mouth. Tears streamed down my face. At that moment, I realized I had been working hard for my parents' dream all along! I knew if I didn't break the pattern of being a people pleaser, doing what was expected of me, the next generation would follow in my footsteps instead of chasing their own dreams.

That conversation led me on a journey of self-discovery. With the help of some amazing mentors, I realized the belief that I wasn't good enough had dictated my life's direction.

In this healing journey of finding my renewed sense of worth, I've learned three profound lessons that have reshaped my understanding of life itself.

Firstly, the transformation we seek in the world must first occur within. Our external realities are merely mirrors reflecting our internal landscapes and perceptions. By reclaiming control over my thoughts, I began to reshape my reality, transforming how I interacted with the world, and, in turn, how it responded to me.

Secondly, I learned the invaluable lesson of forgiveness. We've all been hurt in life, but clinging to that hurt only perpetuates our suffering. I harbored deep resentment toward my father, a society that couldn't see my worth, and the judgment that weighed heavily on me. When we release these burdens—resentment, hatred, jealousy, anger—we not only liberate ourselves from the chains of the past but also open our hearts to compassion and understanding.

Thirdly, I finally understood the profound significance of self-love. The adage, "You cannot pour from an empty cup," resonates deeply with me. To share love and kindness with the world, we must first ensure our own cups overflow. By prioritizing my well-being, desires, and needs, I transformed not only my inner world but also the world around me. Remember, you are the most important person in your life.

This rebirth was not easy! It demanded unwavering commitment, discipline, and perseverance. Emerging on the other side, I can affirm with every fiber of my being that it was unequivocally worth it. I am so proud that I am now living my dream of helping others to break free from their habitual thinking patterns and using the power of their minds to create lives they absolutely love!

My hope is to inspire my children to be the warriors of their dreams. With grace and gratitude, may my story inspire you to discover the resilience within yourself and be a **dream warrior to turn your dreams into reality!**

Alexandra X. Quinn, MPA, CPA is a speaker, business and leadership coach, who is passionate about empowering individuals to break free from habitual thinking patterns. She helps her clients develop inner leadership skills to bring out the best in themselves and others and to achieve their personal, professional and business goals faster and easier.

DreamWarriorsCoaching.com.au

The Art of Work-Life Integration: Lessons from a Mom Entrepreneur

Laura Reale

I was married for a while and struggling to fall pregnant. After years of doctors' appointments and the roller coaster of emotions from the elation that I could be pregnant to the lows of discovering the result was negative, yet again, I gave up. It seemed obvious that the universe had decided to strip me of the privilege of being a mom. This was difficult to accept, especially because friends were falling pregnant at the drop of a hat. To make matters worse, they asked me, "When are you guys starting a family?" To protect my vulnerability, my standard answer was, "When we're ready."

Convincing myself (reluctantly) that motherhood was way down on my priority list, I pursued another dream, that of owning and running my own business. I had grown up in small businesses—my parents and many uncles and aunts also had one. Visiting family meant visiting a store and having coffee and biscuits out the back near the storeroom. If customers came in, anyone could serve them.

I signed a lease twelve months before opening, and as irony would have it, I was five months pregnant. That motherhood urge reignited inside me like a raging fire. I stopped for no one, and the business dream became but a cloud in the far distance. I was ready to let go of the business, but we were so far gone financially that giving up was not an option. I was in a panic, fear running through my veins, when my husband said he'd help—he'd been the one to encourage me to pursue the business in the first place, after all.

The workload was overwhelming. I burned the candle at both ends: the clinic, the paperwork, the long hours, and the sleepless nights with a newborn. Newborn hormones raged through my body taking their toll, and my body crashed. The doctor said that if I didn't put the brakes on, she'd hospitalize me so I wouldn't fall into depression, so my parents took over caring for the baby, and I re-evaluated my priorities.

It was at that moment I made two commitments: one, to be the best mom I could be and run a successful business, and two, to learn as much as possible from the businesswomen and men I met. The idea was to combine these two values no matter what obstacles got in my way. And so, the journey started in what I thought was my way.

Two and a half years later, we had our second child. The elation was huge, but the juggling act intensified. I took the kids to work as often as I could, where their job was to water the plants and clean the leaves.

As the business grew, more challenges appeared. I needed help, so I employed business mentors to assist with the business's needs, but I still had so much more work to do that my family time dwindled even further. Thankfully, I was blessed with a family that looked after the kids, so I knew they were safe and loved.

The work-life balance equation toppled toward work, and I was not happy. Soon, there was a bubbling volcano of conflicting values within me. My gut inspiration surfaced, and I knew what I wanted and what I had to do, but it was not easy.

I continued to take the kids to work. They came with us to important meetings with the promise of a hot chocolate if they behaved, and they "worked" in the stores, organizing price stickers while biting into donuts and custard tarts. My fondest memories are of them entertaining the river of commuters rushing to meet their afternoon trains. Behind closed doors, as we attended to end-of-day tasks, the girls danced, pulled faces, sang, and practiced gymnastics for the people who would smile and wave. It was a show of warmth and humanity in a rushed and serious part of Sydney.

As they got older, they ran errands between stores (we had four by then). I'll never forget the eight phone calls I got from my daughter while walking the ten minutes from one store to the other.

I continued reaching out for inspiration from other businesspeople, which, in the beginning, was all face-to-face. Being an introvert, I crept into the halls and took my seat at the back. To my surprise, the rooms filled up in no time. Women filed onto the stage, telling their stories of how they juggled their values. Some traveled a lot for work, so it was even harder to balance it all. They exposed their vulnerabilities to encourage others and had so many good tips. I immediately bonded and felt as if I had found my tribe.

As the digital age dawned, listening to inspiring people became easier, with podcasts from the comfort of your home at any time of day from all over the world. This was a revolution for connecting people with like-minded goals, and I became obsessed.

There were two light bulb moments. The first was from a woman who'd rejected the term "work-life balance" and replaced it with "work-life integration." Wow! That was exactly what I had been doing, and there was a name for it! My gut inspiration had been right! The second was from a mentor whose teachings involved integrating ALL of life's important areas—family, relationships, career, health . . . whatever is important to YOU—and mapping it all out to make it happen.

After years practicing his combination of journaling and planning, I now do a weekly summary of the most important areas of my life and the weekly tasks I need to fulfill my dreams. Although I never fully complete my plan, it focuses me in the right direction toward a fulfilling life . . . MY WAY.

Know your beliefs, listen to that inner voice screaming for you to unleash that unique ability in you, and don't let conflicting values darken your spirit. Do life YOUR WAY!

Laura Reale *runs Lifestyle Optical, an optical store in the heart of Sydney, Australia, and helps people see well and look good in beautiful frames, sunglasses, and contact lenses. Her goal is to reduce unnecessary blindness and use holistic approaches to eye care, so patients enjoy clear and comfortable vision their entire lives.*

LifeStyleOptical.com.au

WOMEN LEADERS WITH HEALING HANDS

Dr. hc Margareth Reed

The day started like any other day for me. As a teenager, the first thing I did upon waking was to pray. My faith has always been a very important part of my life. This was where I found peace and strength throughout the day and stayed focused on my tasks. Then, I made my bed, had breakfast, and prepared myself to go to school.

Growing up, I was very creative and had multiple interests for my future. I felt a deep desire inside of me to care for ill people, so I played nurse with my dolls, using my mother's needle to sew a wound and put a Band-Aid on it.

My mother was very much into health. We lived near a farm, so everything was organic and fresh. I was taught by my mother to do self-breast exams during my showers as a part of my self-care routine while going through puberty. One morning, as I was gently massaging my breast, I discovered an unusual lump. I was only sixteen years old.

I had never felt that before. My heart was heavy with doubt and fear of what it could be, so I had to tell my mother. Thank goodness she was a proactive woman. She made a preliminary appointment with Dr. Kersaint to see about options. A biopsy was scheduled, and the doctor said we had to have surgery.

I found out that many young teenagers would rather trust a stranger than their parents, but I had no one else to share that with.

I was scheduled to visit with Dr. Kersaint. I asked if I would be able to breastfeed my baby and if I could stay awake to watch the surgery. He agreed. The biopsy was done, the lump was removed, and I had to wait for the result from the laboratory. The waiting period taught me how to be patient.

Finally, the result came back. Dr. Kersaint said it was benign, that I had nothing to worry about, and that I should take good care of myself. The relief was amazing. I felt as if I had a second chance at life.

Later, I realized this was a great opportunity to help other women with self-breast exams regularly for prevention. My scar was a reminder to focus on my purpose. I continued to follow my path in the health care field and secured two patents for the 3Tessla Magnet for Breast MRI patients.

In 2009, I was home on the balcony when I heard a commanding voice say, Go heal My people. Because I was attentive, I quickly registered a nonprofit, but I encountered many difficulties early on, which slowed me down with my passion for helping women in times of need.

In 2016, I heard that familiar voice say, "Breathe," so I took a deep breath in and blew it out.

The voice commanded me to breathe once more. I did. The third time the voice said, "Now, go and help other women breathe again." At that point, I was convinced I had a lot of work to do, and I had to take it more seriously than I had in the past. It scared me.

I did not know how I was going to help women breathe again, but a movement started. In 2018, I invited women to share their stories in an upcoming book anthology with me, and it came to pass in January 2020, with two volumes and twenty-five women's stories published.

Today, I stand here to share my purpose with the world: to help women heal naturally from trauma, to coach women to write their stories, to help them brand themselves, and to breathe again from whatever came to take their breath away.

It took me years to find my healing from within due to childhood trauma, so extending my ability to heal and nurture brings comfort and recovery to those in need as I share my light.

The first step in healing is recognizing the need for it. I compel women to push through their pain and exhaustion. There needs to be a change in mindset to allow healing to take place and bounce back.

True strength lies in acknowledging when one needs support, leading us to the holistic methods we use to address the physical, emotional, mental, and spiritual aspects of women. We are focused on their physical health, their diets, their rest, their energy, and their success.

Mental health teaches them healthier ways to cope with situations, reduce anxiety, manage stress, hone problem-solving skills, and balance their lives to find fulfillment in what they do.

Spiritual health addresses their faith, their resilience, and their perseverance to move forward. Spending time in nature helps focus and foster a sense of peace and belonging.

We address their habits to be healthier, to start writing their stories and strategies, and to overcome barriers from the past blocking their futures.

We inspire hope and positivity to persevere and overcome adversity. We provide guidance and self-image coaching.

We help them find their voices to be unique and authentic, showing up for themselves in their purpose, helping them build their brands, marketing them, and promoting them with speaking engagements, products, and services, and we help them celebrate small victories.

My goal with my organization is to help women to be authentic, to be themselves, to be original, to speak their truths, and not to compromise. As they build their brands and take up speaking engagements, they are ready to empower others to recognize their own potential and capabilities. This empowerment is a form of light, illuminating the strengths and possibilities within individuals and communities from our coaching and counseling programs.

As a *woman leader myself, with healing hands*, through my own experiences, I learned to serve with compassion, wisdom, and empathy. I utilize herbs, spiritual practices, holistic products, services, and approaches to heal and protect my community, and I am happy to serve.

Dr. hc Margareth Reed *is a multilingual speaker, author, coach, and personal branding development expert. She is the CEO of the Women Breathe Again Network, Inc., focused on women's organic healing, offering natural, handmade products, and founder of the Women Breathe Again Holistic Center, Inc., focused on women survivors of trauma.*

WomenBreatheAgain.com and .org

From Resilience to Radiance

Laura Rubinstein

After the engagement breakup, I was left raw and heartbroken. It had been seven years of living with the man I loved. I allowed myself to feel the sadness. Though I could have gone down the victim path of hopelessness and despair, a deep resilience and determination emerged within me saying that blaming others and wanting others to bend to my will was bankrupt. It hadn't worked, and it was not serving me. Ultimately, I realized that no form of trying to go back was going to help matters. I dug into my courage and curiosity and began the spiritual, emotional, and mental health trek of awakening and healing.

The safest place for me to look at all the ugliness I felt inside was in therapy, but just to be sure I was getting to the root cause and could then blossom, I did almost anything supportive to my healing that came my way. I participated in fear-busting programs and grief recovery workshops. I sought out spiritual groups and mentors.

I was stuck until I realized (with the help of those mentioned above) that being a victim of the breakup was a form of self-sabotage caused by fear. Fear had ruled my life for so many years. That's why I stayed in the relationship: I was afraid I would simply create another relationship where I wasn't happy, even though I loved him. I had used fear as an excuse not to move forward.

I had to witness the truth in order to make changes and see different results.

As you might have gathered, I am a rather resilient person. In part, I give credit to my parents. My mother is a mathematician and teacher, and hence, an incredible problem solver. My father always lived by the motto, "No problems, only solutions." This rubbed off on me.

No matter how many problems I solved during this time of my life, I came to realize that problem-solving doesn't bring joy. Problem-solving led me to the next problem to solve. There is nothing wrong with this, and in fact, problem solving became quite handy. However, I wanted to find joy and experience deep love.

At the time of the breakup, I was invisible to men, especially mentally and emotionally available men. In fact, I instant-messaged a guy I had worked with about two years after the breakup. My instant messenger name did not identify me, and he asked who I was when I chimed in. Deciding to be playful, I asked him to guess after telling him we had worked together for five years and, at one point, we were in the same department. He guessed the person in my position before and after me and a few others. When I finally shared a new photo, he still didn't recognize me. When I shared my name, he said, "Oh, wow—I thought you wore glasses." I had transformed and was completely unrecognizable from the former version of myself.

What did I do? I consciously grew my joy. I did not know how to do this, but as I sought answers about how to create a soulful, juicy relationship, various ideas and practices were shared with me. One huge principle I received was that **joy leads to love**. In other words, the notion that finding love would make me happy or bring me joy was a total lie. Instead, the surefire way to have more love was to cultivate joy. It wasn't that hard either, as it turned out. I needed some alternative perspectives and basic practices.

First, I started thinking about what was magical and wonderful in my life as it was. This included the most basic things, such as fresh, clean water. What if I could take a sip, savor it, and appreciate the taste and nourishing effect it had on my cells? Could I actually experience joy? You bet. **Joy is a choice.** When I chose to look at things that were okay or that I liked and added a dose of appreciation, wonder, curiosity, or simply noticed, for a moment, what was so good about the situation, person, place, or thing in my life, I created a joy boost.

Each evening, I wrote five things I appreciated about my day. I also did extra credit and wrote five things I could praise myself for. Oh, and with each statement of gratitude, I paused to feel the appreciation as deeply as I could. These two practices were mind- and life-changing.

It was astonishing. I found my inner dialogue becoming more compassionate and friendly. It oozed out. I became more complimentary, acknowledging, and grateful to others. The result was a ripple effect from positive thinking to feelings of joy and to making more positive choices, and more positive opportunities showed up. This became an upward cycle. At one point, I remember thinking I'd like to be taken to the Olympics in Salt Lake City (after they had started). Two days later, a guy I had met from another city invited me to go, paid my plane fare, and got tickets for several events.

Do you know what happens when you feel so much joy? You radiate. Apparently, that was what I was doing. After my invisible period when I had consciously cultivated this joy, men started following me out of retail stores to sheepishly ask me out. This happened so many times that I had to actively manage which vibes I was sending out.

I became magnetic. Today, I am married to an amazing man, and we have that juicy relationship.

My tenacity and resilience strategy propelled my personal growth, which then guided me to cultivate joy like never before and ultimately transform into a radiant woman.

At the Vancouver Peace Summit 2009, the Dalai Lama said, "The world will be saved by Western woman," but how? I now believe we must cultivate our radiance because it is the power of women in their glorious, radiant selves that inspires change and brings honorable men and women to the table to create a better world for all.

Laura Rubinstein is an award-winning marketing strategist, hypnotherapist, bestselling author of Social Media Myths Busted, *creator of* Feminine Power Cards, *companion book* Journey to Feminine Power, *and* Ignite Your Feminine Soul *retreats for women leaders. She has consulted with 1500+ entrepreneurs to magnetize clients, grow their businesses, and transform their relationships.*

TransformToday.com

Empowered to Rebuild Against All Odds

Emmagness Ruzvidzo

*I came to be through the adversities I was dealt;
adversities my mindset was ill-prepared for. I've had
to rediscover the core of who I am in order to RISE
and become the person I am today.*

On July 20, 2023, I was named one of Queensland's 40 Under 40. Did I see this coming? Not quite. Had I dreamed of a moment such as this? Absolutely!

As we drove home from the awards night, I reflected on the journey that led me here. It wasn't an easy path. It was one filled with resilience, self-discovery, and unwavering determination. I hummed quietly to myself, feeling a profound sense of pride and gratitude.

Six years before, my family and I made a life-altering decision. Leaving behind high-value jobs in Zimbabwe, we moved to Australia, driven by the promise of new opportunities and the desire for a great future for our daughter.

Securing the visa was a rigorous process involving extensive vetting to prove our skills, experiences, and qualifications met the skills gap Australia was facing. With high hopes, I arrived in Australia, eager to start afresh and make my mark in the brand and marketing space.

I've always been extremely ambitious. I grew up surrounded by hard-working women like Maiguru Mpisaunga, Farai Mpofu, Gogo Muchawaya, and my mom, Sekai. These women taught me that excellence was non-negotiable and hard work was always rewarded.

I had worked hard, delivered excellent work, and I was rewarded. By the time I was thirty, I was leading a fifteen-member team as head of retail and marketing.

Within months of moving to Australia, it became apparent that I needed to start my career all over again. Despite my qualifications, I was repeatedly told that I needed local experience. Adding to my frustration, I encountered biases that questioned my place in the marketing field. This felt much harder than a punch in the gut and led me into a spiral of depression. I resolved to keep my head down and just survive.

I learned that pleasing people and being agreeable was my saving grace. Playing small and shrinking myself to fit in meant I could be accepted. I knew from experience that if anyone saw me as a threat, the micro-aggressions and racism would start. I became a shell of my former self within a couple of years.

I got comfortable in a new role and cracked this shell open slightly. Then, I made the mistake of speaking out and adding to the conversation on building a user-centric app. I was immediately put in my place by a senior manager, who retorted to my suggestion, "What does someone from Africa know about digital marketing?" I immediately recoiled and hardened my shell until two conversations helped me step back into my power.

While on a call with my friend, Nyasha, she casually mentioned how my light had deteriorated and that I looked like a shell of the determined, energetic girl she had always known. On a different call, Farai Mpofu asked me why I sounded as if I was whispering and was everything okay? Even my voice projection had lowered to a whisper! This was the wake-up call I needed. I could either remain feeling sorry for myself and just survive, or I could get the help I needed and thrive. I decided to get help.

Life coaching transformed my life! My mindset shifted, and I began to look at life and adversities very differently. Don't get me wrong; the racism, biases, and micro-aggressions were still there, but I decided I wasn't going to let them impact my goals. I had not come all the way to Australia from Zimbabwe to be held back by people who didn't know my story, where I came from, and the impact I wanted to make in this world!

Coaching helped me rediscover my intrinsic motivators and my WHY—the reason I had started my career in brand and marketing, the reason I had moved to Australia: my purpose. Once that realignment occurred, I became unstoppable.

I began to see the value in my unique experiences and contributions. Despite facing the same challenges, I kept moving forward, buoyed by the strength I found in self-discovery and authenticity. My hard work paid off as I began to be headhunted and eventually became the head of brand and marketing for a Fortune 500 company.

As a Black woman (and migrant), my ambition often made others uncomfortable, yet it was my relentless drive and belief in myself that kept me going. The challenges I faced, from magnified mistakes to undervalued successes, were tough to navigate, but I learned to celebrate my achievements, even if it meant advocating tirelessly for myself.

Self-discovery and authenticity became my foundation. I focused on creating value through my unique contributions and communicated effectively to build my professional presence. Networking became my strength, allowing me to build a tribe of supporters and allies. Resilience and empowerment were my guiding principles, helping me stay grounded and focused.

When my dream role was made redundant, I could have easily spiraled, but I didn't break. Instead, I saw it as an opportunity to pivot and pursue something different. My empowered mindset kept me from despair, reminding me of my strength, my purpose, my WHY. This mindset is what I now coach others to embrace, ensuring they, too, can overcome setbacks and embrace new opportunities.

Starting my own business, VAKA Consulting, was a culmination of all my experiences in Australia. VAKA means to build, to lay a solid foundation. The coaching framework I developed—centered around self-discovery, value creation, authentic communication, networking, and resilience—is based on what I've studied as a life coach, my lived experiences, and my professional experience as a brand strategist. My mission is to empower others to find the power within themselves.

This African proverb, shared with me by Elizabeth Lang, is my go-to for empowerment:

> *If there's no enemy within, the enemy outside can do us no harm.*

Emmagness Ruzvidzo *is a multi-award-winning brand strategist, personal brand coach, and speaker. Her journey has helped her build a coaching framework that empowers women and migrants to courageously pursue their goals. With over fifteen years of strategic marketing experience, she helps businesses build iconic brands that deliver results.*

Vaka.com.au

Finding My Purpose: A Journey to Health and Fulfillment

Norva Samuel

"I can do all things through Christ who strengthens me."
—Philippians 4:13

For many years, I wandered through life, grappling with a profound question: what is my purpose? This existential quest wasn't a straight path; it was filled with twists, turns, and numerous challenges that tested my resolve and patience. As time passed, I found myself increasingly insecure and questioning my self-worth. These insecurities grew heavier as I compared myself to my peers, who seemed to have their lives perfectly aligned, ticking off milestones I hadn't even approached.

Throughout this journey, I've worked different jobs and tried various endeavors, experiencing my fair share of failures, yet a common thread was woven through my life: a deep-seated commitment to serving others. This desire to help was a constant driving force that gave me a sense of purpose even when other aspects of my life felt uncertain. My ultimate goal was to serve at a higher level to make a more significant impact in the lives of those around me.

The turning point came amidst a backdrop of personal and familial health struggles. Seeing loved ones battle with health issues was a wake-up call. It forced me to reflect on my own life choices and the direction I was heading. I realized that I was at a crossroads: I could either continue down a path of uncertainty and self-doubt or take decisive action to change the trajectory of my life.

I turned to my faith for guidance. I prayed and asked God for direction and clarity. This spiritual reflection provided me with the strength and resolve to take the necessary steps toward improving my life. In 2022, I made a pivotal decision. I asked myself another simple yet profound question: What's one thing I can commit to that will make life better? The answer was clear and resonant: my health. On April 26, 2022, my health journey began. This date marked the beginning of a transformative period in my life, one that would redefine my identity and purpose.

As a teenager, I had always been interested in weight training, dabbling in it every so often but never committing fully. Until then, my fitness journey had been characterized by years of yo-yo dieting and not being consistent with either exercise or nutrition, and by 2021, I had reached my heaviest weight. The physical weight I carried was a manifestation of the emotional heaviness I felt, years of insecurity, doubt, and unfulfilled potential.

I started with small, manageable changes. I committed to eating better, choosing nutritious foods that fueled my body rather than depleted it. I embraced the importance of daily exercise and understanding that movement is medicine. I began exercising at home, using the space and resources available to me. It was during that time I rediscovered weight training and committed to it with newfound dedication. The act of lifting weights became more than just physical exercise—it was a metaphor for lifting the burdens of my past insecurities and forging a stronger, more resilient version of myself.

Consistency became my mantra. I showed up for myself every day, pushing through moments of self-doubt and fatigue. My home became my sanctuary, a place where I could focus on my growth and celebrate my progress. As the physical weight began to drop, so did the emotional heaviness. Each pound lost represented the release of years of self-doubt and emotional burden. I felt a renewed sense of purpose and self-worth. I was finally facing what was weighing me down. No longer was I the person who questioned their place in the world. I had now become someone who took charge of their destiny.

As I transformed, so did my outlook on life. I realized that my journey was not just about personal gain but about sharing the gift of health with others. My mission to live a life of extraordinary holistic health grounded in faith and continuous personal growth became clearer. I discovered my passion for helping others embark on their health journeys, understanding that a fulfilled life is deeply intertwined with physical well-being. My vision to create a world where holistic health and personal growth are accessible to all drove me forward. I envisioned a community where individuals empowered by faith pursued their wellness journeys, achieving extraordinary health and continual self-improvement.

This mission is rooted in the core values that have become the foundation of my life: health, faith, and growth. Health stands as the cornerstone, essential for every other achievement. Faith provides the strength and resilience to persevere and trust God's wisdom for direction, even when the path is unclear. Growth signifies an ongoing journey toward improvement, strength, and alignment with one's true purpose. It embodies my commitment to continuous personal and collective transformation, fostering a community where well-being and self-improvement are nurtured in every aspect of life.

The journey hasn't been easy, and there have been setbacks along the way, but each challenge has reinforced my commitment to my health and my mission. I have learned that true fulfillment comes not from external validation but from an inner sense of purpose and the knowledge that I am making a positive impact in the world.

Today, I stand as a testament to the power of commitment and the transformative potential of prioritizing health. My journey is far from over, but I am no longer walking in the shadows of doubt and insecurity. Instead, I am stepping forward with confidence, ready to inspire and support women in their pursuit of a healthy, fulfilled life.

Finding my purpose has been a journey of contemplation, commitment, and conversion. It has taught me that we all have the power to change our lives, no matter how overwhelming the challenges may seem. By focusing on our health and embracing health, faith, and growth, we unlock an extraordinary life. It is this journey, this mission and vision, that I am now dedicated to sharing with the world!

Norva Samuel *is a wellness coach and trainer supporting women in pursuing a healthy, fulfilled life. Certified with the Institute for the Psychology of Eating and with Maxwell Leadership, Norva embarks on an enriching journey of personal development, self-leadership, and holistic wellness deeply rooted in spirituality and faith.*

NorvaSamuel.com

Breaking Barriers: A Journey of Resilience and Empowerment in Real Estate

Brigitte Stills

From a young age, I was adventurous, always eager to explore new avenues, and harboring a dream to leave a significant mark on anything I set my heart to. This drive to make a difference fueled my passion and ambition, traits that were put to the test as I embarked on my career journey in the real estate industry. What began as a part-time endeavor quickly blossomed into something far greater than I had anticipated. My initial foray into property management soon transitioned into a successful stint in apartment sales, but my aspirations didn't stop there. I yearned for more—more variety, more challenges, more impact. My ambition wasn't just to sell apartments; I wanted to delve into all facets of real estate. From residential to commercial and industrial properties, I had a yearning to do it all.

Determined to expand my horizons, I scoured the job listings in the local media real estate sections, seeking an opportunity matching my growing ambitions. My persistence paid off when I discovered an opening at one of New South Wales' leading real estate firms, a company renowned for pioneering auction sales both locally and in one of Sydney's most iconic buildings, boasting a network of ten offices. The advertisement called for a sales agent. Notably, it made no mention of gender, signaling an opportunity where my skills and passion could genuinely shine.

After a number of interviews and much perseverance, I joined the company. I found myself in a domain dominated by men, where the only female presence was the receptionist who welcomed visitors. We became good friends. There were instances when our exchanged glances became silent cries for unity in an environment where I often felt overlooked. The process of mastering sales within this office was akin to navigating through a maze without a map. There was no formal training offered; it was non-existent. Instead, I learned through keen observation and the partial answers provided to my constant inquiries. Doubts frequently surfaced, casting shadows over my ambitions and making me question whether I had been overzealous in wanting to join this organization.

While my boss was supportive, my general manager seemed to hold the archaic belief that my rightful place was at home. However, it was the moments of genuine connection with clients whose lives I had the privilege to impact positively that solidified my love for the industry. Whether it was facilitating the sale of a home or managing the lease and rental of their properties, their appreciation made me feel valued and confirmed the significance of my role in their lives. The company acknowledged achievements through various incentives, including a training course in which I found myself the only woman among fourteen men, which both intimidated and motivated me. We sold machinery to each other, bulldozers.

Celebratory events, like dinners or drinks at the Sydney Opera House or similar high-end venues, were also forms of recognition. One such event ended on a night I'd rather forget, when excessive alcohol led to a humiliating fall down the stairs in full view of my colleagues.

The aftermath of that night was the lowest point for me, filled with ridicule and self-doubt. My boss encouraged me to view the situation as a hurdle rather than a setback, but regaining my confidence was a daunting task. My journey through this period was marred by depression, insecurity, and developing an eating disorder, a testament to the toll the experience had taken on my mental and physical health, and I suffered for many years. I refused to attend further celebrations of any kind during my time with the company. I found it hard to trust and communicate with my peers other than for business purposes.

It was the unexpected support from two colleagues, including the once-silent receptionist, that helped me overcome the office politics and backstabbing that hindered my progress. Their guidance revealed the underhanded tactics of my peers, allowing me to transform every lead into a triumph. My hard work culminated in the successful auction of a property that not only exceeded expectations but also served as a personal victory over my insecurities. Local media covered the sale, providing me with exposure to potential vendors and purchasers, and the vendor recommended me to many of his clients.

This achievement marked a turning point, earning me recognition even from those who had doubted my abilities, including a surprising note of congratulations from the general manager. The physical and emotional challenges I faced were significant, leading to time off work and a concerning weight loss. However, my recovery was a journey back to strength and purpose.

In an unexpected twist, the general manager tasked me with mentoring a new female sales agent he had just employed for another suburban office. This responsibility was a profound moment for me. At long last, he saw me as an asset to the organization, reflecting the change I had initiated within the company. It was a change that would pave the way for many women in the real estate industry in that era.

Through perseverance, resilience, and the support of allies, I navigated the complexities of a gender-biased industry, transforming challenges into stepping stones toward success. My journey is a testament to the power of determination and the importance of fostering an environment where everyone, regardless of gender, is recognized for their contributions and potential. Sometimes, the road to success is a hard one to climb; however, the end results can last a lifetime.

To anyone out there doubting their path, remember the words of C. JoyBell C.: "The strength of a woman is not measured by the impact that all her hardships in life have had on her; but the strength of a woman is measured by the extent of her refusal to allow those hardships to dictate her and who she becomes." Your voice is your power—use it, and let your indomitable spirit be your guide.

Brigitte Stills, LREA JP*, is the visionary behind Stills Properties, an independent boutique real estate agency. Brigitte's career spans over four decades, cementing her status as a leader in the real estate industry. She is renowned for her exceptional communication skills, mentoring prowess, coaching, and earning numerous high-achievement awards.*

StillsProperties.com.au

How Free Do You Want to Be?

Andrea Tompkins

*Dedicated to my mother, grandmothers, ancestors,
and generations to come.*

Once upon a time, there was a little girl who lived on the tiny Atlantic island of Bermuda. Life in this idyllic environment lends itself quite well to fairy tales. It's a place dreams are made of, where a little girl's imagination enabled her to create perfect fantasies about what life should look like when she grew up. Childhood experiences and perspectives shaped these fantasies. The unattainable was reinforced over and over again as the video of life playing out in front of her did not live up to the fairy tales created in her mind's eye. Physical, mental, emotional, and spiritual tapes were created inside her subconscious based on faulty thoughts, beliefs, and emotions. These tapes constantly played in the background as blissfully unaware little Andrea went about life in search of the pot of gold at the end of the rainbow, the glass slipper, her Prince Charming, and the sparkling red slippers that would take her home. Every relationship, whether romantic, family, friendship, work, or most importantly, the relationships with herself and her Creator, was run by these tapes. Dreams of the perfect family and marriage, along with sharing her experiences and gifts with the world, were all caught up in the vicious cycle, and none were coming true.

Along came a fellow spiritual traveler who had received the light of Inner Sanctuary meditation, a tool that would end up being one of Andrea's keys to freedom to help her feel less stuck, less frustrated, and less anxious. "Am I not good enough?" she would ask. "What am I afraid of? Failure? Death? What if the worst happens, and I end up alone?" All these fears and more blocked Andrea from living her life to the fullest, from being a mother and a wife, and from loving herself. There was a deep longing and desire within to know herself, the universe, and the stars and to make a connection to the Great Mystery. As a young girl, she sat and stared at the stars and heard her grandmother's voice, her mother's mother, whom she'd never met and who'd crossed over to the other side when her mother was a young girl. Andrea knew she was guiding her from the other side.

On the next leg of her journey, she was guided to travel to what would become her spiritual home in the foothills of the Blue Ridge Mountains of Georgia, USA. As she made her way up the long, winding, tree-filled driveway to the university, there was a familiarity that washed over her before she even realized she had arrived, a recognition, a knowing, a feeling of home, love, and warmth, like a womb.

At this magical place, my spiritual lessons brought me into the unknown depths of self-love and intimacy with Myself and my Creator. One of the many gifts RoHun™ provides is a new perspective. During one of the class discussions, I struggled with a certain energy. Finding it hard to let go and see my part in the situation, one of my beloved teachers, Auntie Janice, simply and eloquently said, "You can keep it if you want," and then she moved on to the next student. I sat in this energy and became more and more uncomfortable. I quickly came to the realization that there was no way I wanted to keep it—absolutely not—in no uncertain terms. This was what I was there for, after all, wasn't it? There, in that far away place, doing all that work—stay stuck? Stay in fear? Stay in pain? Anxiety? Migraines? Absolutely not! Then, a huge shift occurred. That was just one of the magical moments I will never forget during my training.

In the middle of another miraculous RoHun™ session with Auntie Janice, I was brought right into the energy of the migraine. Although extremely uncomfortable, I was able to see how I was confined in the vice grips of the mind. Once I had literally stepped back from the pain in my mind's eye, I was able to gain yet another perspective: to see the cause of the pain and my part in it. I was able to use my wand of light to free myself from the pain, suffering, and faulty thoughts and feelings. Dr. RoHun™ and his team and the teachers who trained me in these powerful processes guided me through the dark night of the soul. I learned we each have the power to clear our own blocks.

RoHun™ Transpersonal Psychology uses spiritual energy to release these blocks with the power of light, transform them into light, and send them back to the universe. The therapeutic process entails working within these constructs of the subconscious mind in order for the client to become free—free to be themselves and live the joyous and happy life they dream of. With my wand of light, guided by God and my dear teachers who held their light for me, I took the journey into the darkest places of my soul and cast out the tapes of fear, death, abandonment, and self-hate. This journey is not for the faint of heart, and it is certainly not for everyone. RoHun™ is for those it resonates with, the warriors of the light. Together, we can be free. We each have our very own wand of light, and we can free ourselves from the bondage of the past—the past of this lifetime and the thousands of lifetimes before this one. RoHun™ can free you from generational cycles and change the trajectory of the lives of generations yet to come. Thank you, Dr. RoHun™ and the Delphi Family of teachers and colleagues. I now carry the light of RoHun™ with me to serve others who are ready to claim their freedom. *How free do you want to be?*

Andrea Tompkins, *a RoHun™ Doctorate Intern, Doctor of Metaphysics, and Integral Master Coach™, is also a two-time bestselling author of* Voices of the 21st Century: Women Transforming the World, *and* Voices of the 21st Century: Women Empowered Through Passion and Purpose. *Andrea lives in Bermuda with her family and works with clients online and in person.*

AndreaTompkins.com

POWER

Power to empower
Myself along with others
Every minute, every hour
Power to achieve the dreams that may be
To master the journey and me
Power to reflect what might have been
And learn from within
Power to shape, with vision so clear
The infinite possibilities that we hold dear

PISSED-OFF CPA ON A MISSION

Ngoc T. Tran, CPA

What if I shared with you a revelation that would shake the very foundations of your financial beliefs? Imagine discovering that the institutions we trust—banks, the Internal Revenue Service (IRS), Wall Street, and Big Pharma—are not the allies we believe them to be. If you had access to the insights I have gained, you would understand why I say this with such conviction.

My background is anything but typical. As a refugee from Vietnam raised by a single mother of eight, I worked full-time while attending college full-time and graduated debt-free. My determination to overcome the poverty that had befallen my family with the fall of Saigon on April 30, 1975, fueled my relentless drive for time, financial freedom, and helping others with similar burning desires.

For much of my adult life, I navigated through the world in blissful ignorance, a corporate zombie following the conventional societal path. I saved for retirement starting at the tender age of nineteen without ever questioning the mechanisms of my 401k, the wealth strategies I employed, or the broader financial, educational, corporate, governmental, and healthcare systems governing my life. I was unaware of the hidden fees in my investments, the limitations on where I could allocate my money, and the ways banks and credit cards took advantage of us. The intricacies of the stock market eluded me, as did the implications of our national debt and government priorities. Even the impact our food, water, and environment had on my health went unquestioned, as did the healthcare system's propensity for legally prescribing addictive and long-term harmful drugs. I was living the American dream, yet I was mindlessly unaware of the realities surrounding me.

My awakening came in stages. The first was in May 2016, amidst the turmoil of a marriage that no longer nourished my soul, leading me to embrace single motherhood and embark on a journey of self-investment and healing. The second was in June 2021, when I stepped away from over two decades in corporate America to dive into entrepreneurship and the insurance industry. It was there that I began to truly understand the "money game" and how the affluent used life insurance for risk-free, tax-free, generational wealth transfer. The final awakening was the understanding that entrepreneurship is a marathon, not a sprint, with pitfalls such as deceit, greed, and misrepresentation that demand resilience, and a steadfast commitment not to abandon our aspirations.

Even as a certified public accountant (CPA) with my expertise in accounting and finance, I came to realize a glaring gap in my understanding of wealth strategies, cash flow management, and the intricacies of financial planning concerning taxes, building generational wealth, and safeguarding assets. This awareness came only after engaging with experts who generously shared their wisdom, allowing me to piece together the bigger picture and connect the dots. I immersed myself in strategic wealth books and valued the critical concepts of the Rule of 72, the power of uninterrupted compounding interest, and the strategies behind capital preservation. Grasping the wealth equation (Money + Time + Rate of Return − Market Risks − Inflation Risks − Tax Risks − Health Costs Risks − Health Care Risks) was pivotal. Understanding this helps devise strategies to counteract these risks and ensure financial stability whether we outlive our savings, die prematurely, or encounter health issues, thereby mastering the nuances of cash flow and the financial game.

Driven by a mission to empower others with this knowledge, I became a "pissed-off CPA," determined to help open-minded individuals grasp the complexities of cash flow and money games. My journey through twenty different businesses taught me to discern which opportunities aligned with my soul's purpose, leading me to create multiple thriving businesses harmonizing wealth and health.

Entrepreneurship is a challenging path fraught with deception, loss, and the harsh reality that most entrepreneurs fail within their first few years. It is through investing in personal development, surrounding ourselves with mentors, creating scalable systems, and leveraging collective wealth creation that we can transcend the traditional trade of time for money. Commit wholeheartedly to mastering your business, not merely showing interest. Cultivate a growth mindset, be resourceful, be open to coaching, and always be ready to engage. Position yourself as a problem solver, maintain focus and consistency, and lead by example with a clear vision and actionable plans for others to emulate. Your belief in your mission and the transformative impact of your endeavors will leave a legacy and change the world. Nurture a deep-seated passion for your work, and never, under any circumstances, give up.

My life's mission is deeply rooted in the desire to enlighten, educate, and bridge the gap in financial misunderstanding. It is about empowering individuals and not only grasping the complexities of financial literacy and applying this knowledge in crafting a life of abundance and intentionality.

If you are still on the path to uncovering your purpose, consider starting with your passions and interests. What lights a fire in your heart and brings you joy? Engage in activities that align with these passions, and pay attention to the moments when you feel most alive and fulfilled. Keep exploring, learning, and growing. Your purpose is out there waiting for you to uncover it and, in doing so, illuminate the path for others.

Ngoc T. Tran *is a certified public accountant, business and wealth strategist, impact speaker, and international bestselling author. As CEO and founder of JJ Capital Partners, Ngoc empowers people to understand their financial health and shares strategies to help them make, save, and protect their money tax-free and risk-free.*

NgocTTran.com

THE POWER OF YES: EMBRACE YOUR FUTURE!

Dr. Anne Marie R. Youlio

What was I doing? Where was I headed? How did everything fall apart?

Three of my four children were out of the house. My youngest was still in high school, but she had her driver's license (i.e., she didn't need my "taxi" services anymore). Everyone was off doing their own thing, living their lives (as it should be). No one told me I'd become an empty nester before they had all left the nest!

I have always worked and had a fantastic consulting business, but family came first. The choices I made and the things we did were based on the family's wants and needs. Don't get me wrong—I absolutely loved all the time I spent with my family. Whether going to sports or plays, chaperoning events, or any other activities, I absolutely loved the experiences. I will always cherish those memories and the family bond we have.

With my newfound freedom and time, I started thinking of activities I wanted to do. How about jet skiing, hiking, or a concert? My husband's response: no, no, and no. Things we used to talk about doing were no longer what he wanted. He preferred to stay home and watch sports. Whoa! That was definitely not where I thought our lives were headed. I felt lost, and I have to admit, in pain.

I kept asking myself, "What about me?"

I read a quote from Tony Robbins: "If you are not growing, you are dying." Wow, that hit home. I didn't know where I was going or what I was going to do, but I had to do something. In my gut, I knew doing nothing was not an option.

I decided I was going to open myself up to opportunities and figure it out. I would say YES to things and see where the yes took me.

I was invited on a trip to Hawaii with some very close friends. Just me. No husband. No kids. While in Hawaii, I spent some time just figuring out what I liked to do. I realized I liked reading, hiking, going for walks, exercising, nature, traveling, and spending quality time with people. I liked experiencing new things. This was a great start! I am a planner, so I started making lists for myself:

- Go to the library.
- Work out at least three times per week.
- Go out to lunch with a friend once a month.
- Try a new activity once a month.
- Try a new recipe once a week.
- Travel once a quarter.
- Expand my consulting business.
- Volunteer.

Did I do all of these things? Of course not! But I had a list to choose from. I was moving forward. I started on this path, and it opened a whole new world for me. I began growing and embracing my future!

I started small, went to the library, and picked up some new books. If I heard someone mention a book they liked, I added it to my list. I later joined a book club. I started going to the gym regularly. I donated blood. I joined a meet-up group that scheduled happy hours, lunches, and other activities and met new people. I scheduled weekends away with friends. I even went zip-lining! This happened over time, but little by little, I expanded my world. And you know what? I found out there were a lot of others out there like me, looking for that experience, that connection, and willing to take that chance!

In the meantime, I had a company approach my consulting firm. They needed somebody with my skill set to be the interim director for an organization while they sought a replacement. The catch? It was located halfway across the country, and they wanted me onsite every week. In the spirit of embracing my future, I said, "Yes." I didn't know how I was going to do it, but I realized that with my additional freedom, I should see where the opportunity would take me. Plus, this was only a preliminary inquiry, and I wanted to find out what was really needed. Well, after further discussion, it ended up that they only needed me every other week. I love traveling, exploring new places, and meeting new people! It was a total win, win, win! While my role with the organization has changed, it has developed into a long-term relationship for which I am grateful! I am so happy I chose to say YES.

If I had chosen to say no, I would have missed out on this amazing experience!

When I reflect on both my personal and professional lives, the best things happened because I said YES. Was it always easy? No. Was it sometimes scary? Yes. But staying in one place, not growing, and slowly dying sounds so much scarier to me that it propels me forward. No matter what, I have to keep trying, keep growing, keep saying YES! Who knows where it will lead me? Isn't that exciting?

I know that I don't have to have it all figured out. I just need to keep taking a step forward. I have learned that how I envisioned my life may not be what happens, but there's something even better down the road for me!

Let's all agree to try something new this week. It doesn't have to be zip-lining (although that was really fun!). Listen to a new podcast, get a new book, decide to go to lunch with a friend, or take five minutes to meditate. Grow into the best version of you! Use the Power of Yes to embrace your future!

Dr. Anne Marie R. Youlio*, PharmD, is the founder of ARDY Consulting, LLC. She has an extensive background in training, strategic planning, and project management within the pharmaceutical and healthcare industries. She is a keynote speaker and serves on the advisory boards to the University of South Florida and the Nvolve mentoring program.*

DrYoulio.com

Turmoil, Tenacity, and Triumph

Jeanne Zierhoffer

In 1989, I hit the lowest point in my life. It was a rollercoaster of emotions: constantly chasing highs only to escape the lows once again. This vicious cycle led to a complete loss of self-identity. Imagine feeling on top of the world, reaching the peak of an insurmountable mountain, only to plummet into despair. Sobriety was just the beginning, and the most painful part was those I loved couldn't rely on me. It was heartbreaking, and I questioned my existence.

November 1989 was a decisive moment for me. It marked the beginning of a long, transformative journey. It was difficult, and I didn't know where to start. So, I began with what was closest to me: my family. I asked for guidance and received the support that allowed me to take the first step toward self-discovery.

I chose to make new friends in new environments, adopt an entirely new lifestyle, and reorganize my chaotic life into one marked by order. Recovery was an unfamiliar journey—a completely new way of living. I am deeply grateful for the few friends who were already on this journey and guided me. Their support made all the difference. I started attending recovery meetings everyday, morning, noon, and night. These meetings helped me stay on track. I moved into a halfway house with twenty-two women for several months, an invaluable support for healing in this community. This experience remains invaluable to this day.

As I continued making life-changing decisions, I developed an unwavering commitment to life. After about two years of attending recovery meetings several times a day, I had an eye-opening realization. There was a fear instilled at some of these meetings—the fear of relapsing if I stopped attending them. This fear made me question whether I was merely replacing my addiction with an endless cycle of meetings. Constantly attending meetings wasn't the quality of life I wanted. If that was the case, I might as well have continued using drugs and alcohol. So, I chose to identify as a "recovered addict," not a "recovering addict." The label "recovering" kept me tethered to the past. Being "recovered" meant moving forward and truly living the life I desired. The recovery meetings provided a roadmap to my new life, but living in constant fear of relapsing kept me focused on exactly that: relapsing. Recognizing that what you focus on expands, it became clear to me that I wanted to focus on further developing the map of my new life!

In my pursuit of a harmonious and joyful life, I reduced my meeting attendance to twice a week, freeing up time, energy, and space to secure a job. I transformed into a trusted member of my community, taking a role at the local bank as a teller. This job greatly enhanced my ability to connect and communicate effectively with others.

This led to an even greater life event: getting married and building a life and home together. It felt like a dream come true. As we built our new life and dreamed of starting a family, I remembered that children are sponges, observing and learning from their parents' actions and behaviors rather than words. This awareness ignited a deep desire to become the best mother and wife I could be. I embraced my role as a mother, maintaining a clean house, cultivating a flower garden, holding down a job, and, most importantly, being an active part of my kids' lives.

Desiring more time-freedom and flexibility, I decided to become a real estate agent, beginning my entrepreneurial journey. I had to quickly learn how to juggle all the responsibilities that now filled my life. Within a few years, I became one of the top producers and income earners in our local residential real estate market. Balancing my kids' activities and responsibilities while being a parent and business owner often made our household chaotic. Fortunately, I married the right person. John was man enough to quit his job to spend time with the kids, allowing me to focus on my real estate career.

One specific day remains vividly etched in my memory. School was closed due to snow, and I was on the phone with an attorney, managing multi-million-dollar homes. Glancing outside, I saw my son flipping over on his four-wheeler in our front yard. I quickly hung up the phone, rushed outside, and heard both boys laughing, all bundled up in their snowsuits. They had a chain and proceeded to flip the four-wheeler over again; they were having the time of their lives! This memory, among many others, serves as a reminder of my priorities: family first.

In that moment, I took stock of myself: "Who am I?" I answered myself: I am a mother and a real estate broker running my own business for my family. I'm a wife, a daughter, a sister, a housekeeper, and an accountant. The many hats I wore daily led to an identity crisis. My journey involved mastering the balancing act between my career and my family, all while cherishing the support of my husband.

One moment, I wore my real estate hat; the next, I was the Little League baseball coach. Ten minutes later, I became the librarian mom, then back to showing houses, and finally home, cooking dinner. The balancing act never ends; the constant shifting of roles and identities is part of my evolution, leading to personal growth. My life's motto is to check my worries at the door and be fully present. When coaching Little League, business worries are left at the field's edge. Business matters have no place at the dinner table.

This transformation isn't just about me; it's about being part of a supportive network that values integrity and mutual respect. By committing to positive change, I've improved my own life and strengthened the fabric of my community. Standing together in our collective power, especially in moments of vulnerability, has allowed me to build an amazing team and a thriving business.

Jeanne Zierhoffer is the "Implementation Queen," transforming complex strategies into simple action steps, empowering women to identify, implement, and achieve infinite success. She is known for her authentic, systematic, and results-driven approach as a certified professional NLP coach and sales trainer.

LinkedIn.com/in/JZierhoffer

BOOK CLUB CONVERSATION STARTERS

This book, *Voices of the 21st Century: Wise Women Bringing Light to the World*, contains the stories of women from around the world who have persisted through dark times and found their way to light. These stories illuminate the wisdom that saw them through and continue to elevate their lives and the lives of others. Allow their wisdom to amplify yours as you explore the following questions with your book club members:

1. After reading these stories of wise women who bring light into the world, who are the wise women who have been present in your life? How did they enlighten you?

2. Which of the stories brought you to tears? Laughter? Deep thought? What, in particular, brought up these emotions?

3. What is important about women bringing their wisdom and light into the world? Since reading these stories, are you more aware of how you bring light into the world or want to?

4. What current causes and issues would benefit from wise women bringing light to them? What organizations might you support or get involved with?

5. What next steps are you inspired to take? How might you do that in collaboration with others?

6. If you were to write a story, chapter, or book, what would you write about? What impact would you like it to have on others?

7. Given your passions and the areas you are wise about, how will you bring light to your family, community, region, etc.?

WHAT IS YOUR STORY?
If you'd like to share it within a collective like this book, visit **VoicesOfThe21stCentury.com** to find out how you and/or your group can participate.

VOICES OF THE 21ST CENTURY

A collection of empowering stories by women from around the world sharing, insights, hope, wisdom and inspiration.

Women Who Influence Inspire and Make a Difference

Bold, Brave, Brilliant Women Who Make a Difference

Powerful, Passionate Women Who Make a Difference

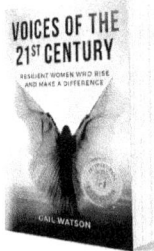
Resilient Women Who Rise and Make a Difference

Conscious, Caring Women Who Make a Difference

Women Transforming The World

Women Empowered Through Passion and Purpose

Meet the authors and read their bios at: **voicesofthe21stcenturybook.com**

available at

HAVE A MESSAGE TO SHARE?

Whether you're a speaker, author, or poet, the Women Speakers Association has meticulously developed comprehensive guides to elevate your journey. Explore our Speaker, Author, and Poet Success Plans to boost your voice, increase your visibility, and engage with a supportive community. These complimentary, expertly crafted plans are your gateway to discovery and achievement.
Your message matters!

Start Your Journey with These FREE Guides

SPEAKER SUCCESS PLAN
Amplify your voice, elevate your platform, and connect with audiences globally.

SpeakerSuccessPlan.com

AUTHOR SUCCESS PLAN
Transform your words so they have impact, gain visibility, and become a published author.

WSAPublishing.com

POET SUCCESS PLAN
Share your poetry, inspire the world, and join a community of creative voices.

PoetSuccessPlan.com

www.ingramcontent.com/pod-product-compliance
Lightning Source LLC
LaVergne TN
LVHW012151090325
805543LV00031B/789